EXPERIENTIAL EDUCATION:

XED

How to Get Your Church Started

JOHN & LELA HENDRIX

ABINGDON PRESS
Nashville and New York

Experiential Education: X-ED

Library of Congress Cataloging in Publication Data

HENDRIX, JOHN. Experiential education, X-ED. Bibliography: p. 1.
Religious education. 2. Church group work.
I. Hendrix, Lela, joint author. II. Title.
BV1471.2.H45   268   75-4722

ISBN 0-687-12421-2

*Dedicated to
Melissa and Jud
Not only our children,
but children of Life.
They taught us to play.*

. . . I would tell a tale of God calling His human children to form a great circle for the playing of His game. In that circle we ought all to be standing, linked together with lovingly joined hands, facing towards the Light in the centre, which is God ("the Love that moves the sun and the other stars"); seeing our fellow creatures all round the circle in the light of that central Love, which shines on them and beautifies their faces; and joining with them in the dance of God's great game, the rhythm of love universal.

D. M. Baillie, *God Was in Christ*

CONTENTS

ACKNOWLEDGEMENTS

The common meal (p. 78) was first introduced to us by Meg Robertson.

The Patio Conversation Dinner (p. 145) is a creation of several people but primarily two "Anns," Ann Lee and Anne Guy.

The Place (p. 132) demanded the coordinated efforts of many people. Gene Wright, Bruce Powers, and Oeita Bottorff were the "catalysts."

1 THE CONVERSATION

Tom and Martha Phillips, Paul and Sandy Johnson, and Richard and Ann Hollander are old college classmates. They still get together several times each year for a weekend. They are all in their late thirties with children of various ages. Tom and Martha, and Paul and Sandy live in the suburban area of a large city and go to the same church. Tom owns a gasoline station, and Martha stays at home with two preschoolers. Paul is an architect, and Sandy teaches in a local elementary school. Richard, who is a pharmacist, and Ann live in a county seat town in a neighboring state, and on this particular weekend they are the hosts for the other families.

PAUL: Well, it's a new day in our church. Two weeks ago the four of us attended a seminar with about fifteen other couples in our church. Frankly, I never expected to be in anything like it. In fact, if someone had told me what we were going to do, I probably wouldn't have gone.

ANN: Paul, I've seldom seen you so excited about your church life. What happened?

PAUL: Well, the seminar was held in our church dining hall. The church council had decided to have a workshop for the adult leadership. Our pastor is a friend of a "minister of groups," or some such title, in a church in another city. This friend was invited over for a four-day seminar. He would be sort of an outside "third party" who could help us look at ourselves and our communication patterns.

MARTHA: We walked in that first Sunday night and I was surprised right away. Someone had said that we were going to meet in the fellowship hall, but when we got there the chairs were arranged around the wall and the room was open, empty space. I thought there had been a mistake so we went on to the sanctuary. But sure enough, we were planning to meet in the dining hall.

TOM: And there we were, sort of nervously sitting there looking at each other wondering, *What in the world is going on?* At the beginning the guest leader asked us to invest as much of our lives as possible in the four nights and make it a priority concern during that week. Then he asked us to think of the dining hall as a living environment. He said we were going to be spending about twelve hours in this place. He talked about really getting acquainted with all the "living" space—like we were joining a caravan and were going to be journeying together for a long time. He talked about getting everyone on board before we began the journey.

SANDY: I remember getting kind of anxious. I thought to myself, *What does he want us to do? How am I going to look in front of all these people?* He asked us to walk around the room and get acquainted with all the space and the people in that space. But he asked us not to talk while we were doing it. I couldn't help giggling at first. It all looked so silly. But then I realized that I was really seeing the room and those people for the first time. And these were people I've been in church with for five years! It was strange, like walking downtown where you don't know anyone. But I was beginning to get a picture of all of us on a journey together somewhere.

PAUL: After we had moved around the room for about five minutes we were asked to group ourselves with six or seven other people and mark out our own little space in the room for the next four nights. He described it as an environment—our space and our people.

SANDY: Up to this time I really didn't know what was going on, but I seemed to be having fun so I just stuck with it. The time passed really quickly, and I was surprised when an hour had gone by. We were involved in all kinds of different activities, and something about them reminded me of recess back on the old playground at Fairmount Elementary School. Yet, it was different here. We would play a game, and then sit down and talk about what we'd done. We played with an imaginary ball; we imagined ourselves using a baseball, a football, marbles, and even a bowling ball. I was one of the pins! Then we'd sit down and talk about what had happened.

MARTHA: Yes, I'll never forget those three things he kept asking us all week—"How do you feel? What happened? What did you learn?"

PAUL: As I look back on it, the last hour of the first night was critical for me. I really was beginning to feel that I wasn't going to come back. And it would have been all over before it got started. Those first exercises were all right—a little fun—sort of ice breakers, I guess. Then I thought, *Now he'll get down and tell us what we're supposed to be doing.* But it was just the opposite of that, and I really began to get confused. All sorts of things began to run through my head. *Why am I here? Why am I doing this? I'm not getting anything out of this.* There are all those things I've been waiting to do in my workshop at home. You see, I have always been used to going into church, sitting down, and listening to someone talk. But here were a new set of questions:

"What did I want to learn?"

"Why was I here?

"Was I willing to participate in the setting of goals and attaining them?"

I had never been in a group that had asked me those questions.

TOM: I've been thinking about those questions, too. I realize that I was totally unprepared in knowing how to respond. In fact, they didn't make sense. I was so conditioned to other ways of learning. I realized I had never accepted an active role in defining what a group was going to do. But now at this seminar there were no boundaries set on what was going to happen other than those I set on myself. And that was a new experience?

PAUL: Well, look maybe I can say it this way. Richard, what comes to your mind when I say I've had a learning experience.

RICHARD: Well, I think of a teacher and a classroom.

ANN: And a textbook.

PAUL: Right! That's the way most of us think. The teacher is the expert and we listen. We do well when we learn what he is trying to teach. The ideas and concepts come from a book. The classroom assumes that learning is a special activity set off from the rest of life. But the style we used those nights was different. We are all teachers and learners. We learn best from life's experiences and then any place becomes a place for learning.

MARTHA: After the first two nights I was much more comfortable with the process and I began to experiment more with some ideas. *I was trying out new roles, testing new rules.* I was discovering how this new process worked. I would really like to try some of those exercises again. They happened so quickly and I've been thinking about so many different things that I'd like to see what happens a second time around. It's as if you see things for the first time. You not only see and hear with your eyes and ears, but you get the feeling that you're understanding with your feet and hands. Your whole body wakes up and comes alive. Do you remember the preacher talking about the Bible being the "living word." I think I understand that now. Anything that's true must come alive—in us!

TOM: The seminar leader asked us what we had learned that we could use some other time. And he mentioned that *if these exercises were the real world of experience, what would they be teaching?* I'll tell you what I learned. I don't think I can ever go back to making decisions for people and trying to get them to buy what I had decided.

The process of involving people really became important to me. The main message in the whole seminar was that we all have a unique contribution to make and all parts fit together in a meaningful way. Do you recall studying I Corinthians 12 in Sunday school? We read the verses again in our group, and it was like hearing them for the first time. You've got to experience the concept before you understand it fully! I can really begin to see what happens to a bunch of people who are a team. You talk and practice, talk and practice, talk and practice. There's no one person making all the decisions. In fact, in our group everyone was the leader at some time. I discovered that leadership switched around as different people had things to offer.

MARTHA: The times of reflection were most meaningful to me. I discovered that my patterns of thinking were old and tired. I thought, *Here is a new world, and I am trying to get acquainted with it.* It dawned on me that I knew some things that I had forgotten or didn't know I knew. Do you understand what I mean? After we had been involved in a group experience something would leap before my mind—something someone had said or something I had read that suddenly made sense. I guess they call it insight. I know I've got some new understandings of the parables of Jesus. But it was like some unknown portion of myself emerging that was there all the time, yet hidden from me and everyone else.

SANDY:Most of those games were like real life experiences, and *I began to look at life in a new way.* What problem did I face? How did I attempt to meet the problem? How was I affected by the results? How could I have dealt with it in a better way? How has God used that experience?

PAUL: Yeah, and even the work became fun in this seminar. I discovered that these *new principles could be applied to real problem situations.* On the last day we talked about setting up some priorities for our teaching this year. I didn't think that all of us could possibly come to some major decisions on objectives. Always before when we've tried to have a large planning meeting, we've ended up in a big powwow with some people getting mad and some others just throwing up their hands. But this time we started out with some work sheets to use as we developed some goals for our teaching. I jotted down some things and discussed them with the other people in my group. I ranked my five priorities and then talked with a couple of other people in my group. We were able to agree on three priorities. Finally, we batted the ideas around the whole group of eight people until we could all agree on five priorities. Then all these priorities from the different groups were written on newsprint which was mounted on the wall for all to see. We went back into our groups and talked some more. Do you realize that at the end of the morning we had set up five major goals for our teaching during the next year and some strategies for getting at the goals. And everyone was supporting each other. It was because we worked toward a shared agreement—consensus, I think that's what the leader called it.

SANDY: It's just a different way of looking at things. It's always asking the questions of what's happening here and how do I feel about it. I used to save all my comments about what happened at church for talking in the car on the way home. But the leader kept saying, "Whatever you would say about your group, say now." That puts everything on the table, so to speak. The idea is to involve people instead of to make decisions for them. It's really developing a team spirit. I've even got some new ideas I'd like to try with some adults and children together.

MARTHA: Do you remember the large poster in one corner of the room? That poster told the secret to the whole seminar. It said:

Tell me—I'll forget
Show me—I'll remember
Walk with me—I'll understand

Authors' Note

The above conversation is an illustration of the kinds of questions people ask when they first enter X-ED, experiential education. This is what really happens sooner or later, consciously or unconsciously, when people begin a new style of learning. Leaders of gaming and learning exercises who do not realize this fact can become easily disillusioned. Those leaders that know and forget will often be reminded by the responses of people.

At first there is a natural anxiety created by a new situation. This is a period of orientation. Some people never move past the stage of "Why am I doing this?" Secondly, there is a period of experimentation as persons seek to become comfortable with a new process. Finally, there is a direct application made to a person's unique life situation. A person may be operating at more than one stage simultaneously; but if early questions are not resolved, they will be carried forth in subsequent stages. (The italicized parts of the conversation illustrate the thoughts that occur as people become acquainted with this new learning experience.)

2 THERE IS NO LONGER A FRONT OF THE ROOM

"You get to be a teacher and you build something in the room. Students push it around; maybe you push it around. It starts to show stress, begins to fall apart. You fix it up or start over again. You learn something. Students learn something. And sometimes you get a break, a treat, a real feast day in class when a student, or a couple of students, or the whole class builds something in the room; and you push, and push, and push and it works."

—Jon Wagner, *The New Teachers*

Introduction

It begins with looking at a room in a different way. The rows of seats, faced one way, with a desk and clean blackboard do not make sense anymore. It is not much fun looking at your own feet or at the back of the person sitting in front of you. Learning is fun when it is "cozy"—knees to knees, nose to nose. What happens when there is no longer a front of the room? There is just a room filled with people, and air, and space, and light, and windows, and walls. What happens is that *everything* in the room has potential to teach. Out of this change in perspective comes the basic principles which provide the foundation for this book.

1. We are responsible for our own learning, and we generate the learning process in others.
2. We learn from our mistakes and those of others.
3. We are involved in face-to-face transactions with others—giving, receiving, offering, resisting, and sharing.
4. We make the most out of the present—the time, the place, and the people. "At all times and in all places" is the Christian's response to life.
5. We learn best when we have a part in planning the learning activity.
6. We each have a unique learning style that may differ slightly or radically from others.
7. We learn best when that which is to be learned becomes immediately useful to us.
8. We know that motivation for learning is difficult and complex. However, we learn what we want to learn. Each person is responsible for finding the will to want to learn. Leadership must provide learning opportunities.
9. Learning is playing because we are free people, given all things to enjoy (I Tim. 6:17-19).
10. We learn when the next step forward is more joyous and spiritually satisfying than that which has become familiar or even boring. When an experience is delightful then we want to return to it, repeat it, and savor it. Each new experience validates itself!

BEGINNINGS

Games are not new to the church's educational experience. They have always been an expression of the religious life of a people. Games had a way of picturing the struggle of life between the old and new order, good and evil, life and death. Often the conflict was expressed in combat or a ceremonial contest. A tug of war, race, athletic feat, dance, or theatrical performance "showed the world" that the forces of destruction were overcome, and that the forces of Christ were victorious once again.

The ancient game of chess was designed to enable players to learn the strategies and tactics of warfare. Chess, as it developed in Europe, became a simulation of the political, social, and religious structures of the Middle Ages. From their earliest beginning, games were used as devices to train people for good performance in combat.

Complex learning games were in existence as early as 1800. The modern emphasis on games began in business and industry during the 1950s while developing exercises for management training. People naturally think that games are most helpful in working with children and adolescents. *But the origin of learning games was related specifically to a learning methodology for adult education and training.*

DEFINITIONS

Experiential education can be traced to several traditions. Simulations, games, role-playing, improvisational theater, and learning exercises and instruments have all influenced this new movement in teaching. All these methods, used in small groups, are basic building blocks of experiential education. The focus is on the total environment, much like a home teaches through everything that goes on within its walls. Persons are seen as an organic whole. They influence one another and work toward mutual purposes and goals (I Cor. 12 and Eph. 4). Because of the similarities and interrelation of these learning techniques some definitions and clarifications are in order.

1. Simulations

The word "simulate" has its roots in biology. As the body takes in food it appropriates all sorts of substances into the body tissues: blood, bone, skin, muscle, nails, and hair. This process of changing dissimilar things to similar things is in the root word *assimulare.* Hence the words "simile," "similar," "simultaneous." To simulate is to create a situation that is lifelike, that is like something else. A simulation is an educational tool for helping people learn by experiencing in a different way their daily situations. Simulator trainers illustrate this definition. A pilot trainee may learn to fly an airplane by use of a simulator which provides the appropriate visual vehicles of a runway, and informs him whether he is too low, too high, or off center. If real planes were used, practice landings would be hazardous, not to mention expensive. The computer-controlled simulator provides the experience of flying, without the hazard. The attempt here is to allow the trainee to experience in a learning situation what he eventually has to experience in real life. Some aspects of reality are omitted while other aspects are brought into focus.

The importance of simulating experiences is illustrated well in the statement of a former Air Force bomber pilot who compared an educational simulation with his pilot training. "In twenty years as a pilot. I suffered only two major crises from which to learn. I lost two engines. Over the years in the Link trainers and more modern aircraft simulators, I have lost four engines, crashed twice, and died once. Simulators offer some distinct advantages as environments in which to learn from experience."[1]

2. Games

Games may be thought of as competitive encounters between individuals that involve some degree of skill or luck. Games are usually looked upon as pleasant or even stimulating diversions from other, more meaningful, activities. "Serious" games involve people in gainful competition, but winning or losing is not valued as much as the learning involved in the experience. In most instances a game is a marketed product that uses a playing board, troops, money, votes, or tokens as teaching tools.

Almost any department store now features a consumer area that was not there five years ago. The displays will be identified as "adult games." The games are attractively packaged and range in price from $2.00 to $300. or more. The field of adult education is expanding daily, and learning games can be found on practically any subject.

3. Role-Playing

Role-playing may mean the same thing as sociodrama, which refers to a technique that involves groups in "pretending" or play-acting. Role-playing is an unprepared, unrehearsed dramatization and works toward the development of deeper understandings and relationships. In role-playing the actor assumes another's identity and must make decisions about that assumed identity. In simulations the student steps into a situation in which he, as himself, must make decisions, bringing all his convictions, skills, and experience to bear on the problem.

4. Action Parables

Robert Dow in *Learning Through Encounter* describes the "action parable" as one form of experiential education. He takes this concept from the parables found in Jesus' life and ministry. Parables are both spoken and acted out. The spoken parables are obvious in the teachings of Jesus, but they are sometimes difficult to interpret because they require reflective skill that includes an open, searching mind and an awareness of metaphors and similes. The action parable is more direct. It is an encounter, a confrontation which involves all the senses: sight, hearing, smell, touch, and taste. It is multidimensional as a communication process.

The action parable is real, concrete, and observable. It may take only two or three minutes, which is a much shorter time than is needed for most simulations and games. It is a teaching tool that is spontaneous, descriptive, and relevant to life. It is a slice of life. Dow suggests six characteristics of an action parable.

1. It is simple—single in its objective.
2. It is concrete—descriptive in its nature.
3. It is relevant—strongly attached to the hearers daily life.
4. It reflects the common life, but in an uncommon framework.
5. It has many ramifications beyond the intended purpose.
6. It leaves the response up to the learner.[2]

SPACE IS HOW YOU FILL IT

The first barrier toward experiential education is in assumptions made about space. The old dictum is true—"We shape our buildings, thereafter they shape us." In other words, architectural forms are allowed to restrict and determine the boundaries of our involvement. Fixed space becomes another way of predicting and controlling the activities of people. Unconsciously we let our surroundings define what we are going to do. But these settings are often unhelpful and detrimental to what we are trying to do.

Needs and settings are not always coordinated, since our needs change faster than our settings.

One might feel that there are more important things to worry about other than the architecture of the room. But new learning environments cannot be created until this issue is settled. *The lack of disciplined followers who are equipped for ministry is directly related to assumptions we have made about space.* For our settings often concentrate the attention of the many on the few, and thrust the many into rows of spectators rather than participants.

When we say there is no longer a front of the room, we mean that we are ready to make new statements about teachers, classrooms, and the learning process. The biblical patterns of "a people on the way" pictures a team approach, people banded together for a common cause. Strength is found in the performance of all the people and is valid only as it is in process—on the way toward the kingdom. Most churches have been designed for private experience—settle down, sit, and listen. But biblical images show man in motion with an inner urging to be free, to travel, to be called out, to be on the way.

The type of learning process suggested in this book creates and uses space. The walls and enclosures must be seen as holding a dynamic and energetic process. As one architect puts it, "Of all buildings the church building must be the sort which says to the people who gather, 'you are the important things here. You are the temple of God. I am not.' The nature of the shelter in its scale, its light, color, texture, and space must be lovingly subservient to the community of persons it serves."[3]

The first step is to become aware that buildings provide alternate ways of using space. Some features are relatively nonchangeable and nonmovable—load-bearing walls, floors, and seating arrangements which are fastened to the floor. Whenever seating arrangements are fixed and unmovable, some designer has not understood learning environments. To pick up a phrase from Vernard Eller, "pews have given the church a bad odor."

Often the problem is "pseudo-fixed space"—space that is simple to change or redesign, but which is seen as fixed even when it is inappropriate to learning situations. In many settings there are changeable features which often are treated as if they were fixed. Flexible space does not automatically make an environment more dynamic, but it does make possible the use of variations in bringing the potential richness out of the setting. How do we go about changing our environment for a more exciting learning process? Here are some suggestions:

1. Become more aware of our own learning environments. What is our setting causing us to do? Do we let it define what we are going to do?
2. Continue to ask, What are we trying to do here? Is the setting appropriate for what we want to experience and accomplish?
3. Determine how we can use or change the setting to communicate more closely the meaning of the Christian message. Will a change in location provide a better fit between content and process?

WHAT IS MEANT BY "LEARNING FROM EXPERIENCE"?

If the gospel is true and if it means what it says, then it is happening in someone's life at a deep, experiential level. When the gospel's truth touches what is true about the deepest part of ourselves, the gospel becomes the living word. Words and lives come together. Persons become a truth, rather than simply knowing words that are true. In spite of what one might observe, the Christian life is not talk. Words are the vehicles for communicating experience. But truth must be lived before it can be really known.

Uncle Remus said, "Experience is what you get when you stop listening to your Ma and Pa." And so it is. Learning is experiencing the truth in our own way and not the way we were taught. Think of a cone with the point at the top. The top of the cone provides learning methods from the experience of others. The base of the cone uses methods that utilize the learner's experience.[4]

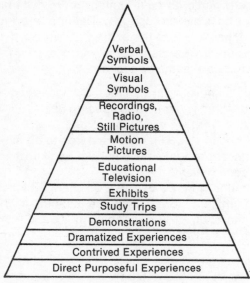

The cone of experience includes a comprehensive range of learning experiences that should be a part of any learning design. These experiences are not separated entities because each is enhanced with exposure to methods from other areas. The position on the cone determines the depth and breadth of the method in terms of direct experience. The higher levels of the cone are more dependent on the experience of others, and therefore more restricted in terms of personal experience.

Direct purposeful experiences involve the senses, minds, and bodies. They include the freedom of creating an idea, designing a plan, pulling together the resources and assuming the responsibility for putting all the parts of the project together.

The further down the cone that one gets, the more the methods depend on the imaginative involvement of the learner. The methods and processes suggested in this book are intentionally designed to direct a person toward the base of the cone.

WHAT HAPPENS TO PERSONS?

The primary behavior resulting from experiential learning has been the intense involvement of the participants. Complete absorption in an activity, to the point of being oblivious to other events, is often observed. "I have never felt so affirmed in my life." "I have never received so much insight in such a short time." "I was so involved that I forgot the time." After one three-hour session, group members reported that they stayed up talking about it until 3 A.M.

Persons often report that their perceptions and understandings of others have changed considerably. Changes have been seen in attitudes toward learning, other people, groups, men and women, and the particular subject content of the experience. Interest in theology, ethics, and church history increased noticeably through experiential education.

Expressions of personal satisfaction, distrust and trust, a need for dominance, a need for structure, and a request for support are frequent and visible during play. Persons discover that life is often more complicated than they ever dreamed. They also discover they know things which, up to that moment, were never brought to awareness. Insight is sharper, listening and speaking are more intense, decision-making and problem-solving skills are more precise and accurate.

Experiences of community and group spirit are heightened. Learning is relational, face-to-face, back and forth, testing strengths and weaknesses. There is a rhythm and a flow of energy between the participants. The hilarious, the frivolous, and the serious are all part of a shared experience.

Even though a game is played several times the patterns of interaction and the results differ with each playing. Children know this when they say, "Do it again." They are really saying, "I missed something the first time around. I'd like to try it again." Experiential education involves the whole person. It does away with the process of education that tries to separate and divide learning goals into neat structures, often neglecting the integration of a total learning experience.

WHAT ARE THE LIMITATIONS?

There are some negative aspects and limitations. Although the consensus of evidence points to great values, there are some limitations.

1. Often churches are not designed for experiential educators. The redesign of space is crucial. A large, open area with flexible seating arrangements is needed. Sometimes a large, open area with no chairs is best.
2. Gaming sometimes intrudes on other groups in the building. This "learning noise" often introduces considerable changes in talking, laughing, and physical movement.
3. Intense competition may develop between opposing players and teams. Allegiance and loyalty to the team become more important than learning. Team experiences must be balanced with total group involvement and learning.

4. Persons who need a high degree of structure and order may find a typical learning game confusing. A mistake is made in assuming that everyone is ready for experiential learning. Some people are not! Many persons can be won over, but it may be in the face of much hesitancy. Resistance can be expected along the way.

5. Published games are sometimes expensive, both in terms of cost and in the time they take to use. Games should have multiple uses with several age groups before a lot of money is invested.

6. Learning is often difficult to evaluate. Behavioral changes appear only gradually, and the influence on the deeper levels of experience does not appear immediately.

7. Do not expect miracles. Games and simulations *might* produce learning, however, they are not cure-alls for a dead program, so add them to a rich list of other methods.

DESIGNING SIMULATIONS, GAMES, AND LEARNING EXERCISES

The leader of a simulation/gaming experience must see himself as a designer of environments. The leader provides an atmosphere. In fact, the leader *is* an atmosphere. He shapes the space and time elements of the learning situation. He guides the content-involvement-reflection experience. An analogy is the role of a playground director during recess. The director describes the game, assigns the players, sets the rules and boundaries, and gets the game started. He is often a voice on the sidelines—encouraging, urging on, and suggesting new tactics and strategies. He knows that there are many ramifications beyond just "playing the game." Sideline coaching by the leader is a vital part of the structured experience. Since everyone is in the game, the leader is often the only cheering section. "Concentrate!" "Make it real!" "Play hard!" "Work it out!" These are frequent examples of this cheering, encouraging process.

The leader's goal is the participation of all persons present, at whatever level they are most comfortable. He works best as a facilitator, a helper. As a helper, the leader may play many roles—coach, enabler, referee, scorekeeper, timekeeper, organizer, observer, model participant, commentator. A good leader is able to use any of these styles, and more, depending on what is needed.

As people become more comfortable with the process, the leader may be able to become more of a participant. As a member of a group he expresses his views as those of one member only. The leader's words do not carry any more weight than those of others. But he does not ask others to do what he is not willing to do himself.

Again, Jesus is the example of the master designer of environments. He used everything around him to teach— the place, the time of day, the people, the children, the clothing, the soil, the trees, the lunch of a boy, grains of wheat, and a Roman coin. With these things he shaped a learning situation.

There are several vital steps in experiential training design. Although not all experiences will have all these elements, they will have many of the following.

1. Carefully define your goals and objectives. What do you want to teach, or what does the group want to learn? Make your goals realistic and concrete.
2. Define space and time allotments. In other words, what are the length of the game and the boundaries of the playing field? Remember, there is no front of the room.
3. Construct a model (image or picture) of the process

or system that will best serve the objectives. How can we best picture what we want to learn? The model should be simple, concrete, and flexible.

4. Determine the size of the teams and the number of teams to be involved. Most groups can accommodate six to ten people. This brings greater variety and makes the experience more involved and animated.

5. Define the roles in each group. What are individuals to do and what are they working toward? Are persons acting separately, or are they working toward a group goal?

6. Determine the resources available to each member of the team. Are they group resources or personal resources? Do they have talents, votes, money, or tokens to use in cooperation or in competition with other players? How can persons utilize their own experience to best effect? Other materials may include a sheet of paper with a role-playing situation, or they may include the design of a game board, chance cards, or score sheets.

7. Determine the interaction sequence between the players in the group. What is to be done with the flow of resources and information to and from each person? What are some of the possible consequences of their behavior? Will they gain theological understanding, ethical insight, economic advantage, group cohesiveness, social advantage, prestige, status in the community, personal growth, power, or *what?*

8. Set limits on permissible behavior including time limits, and what can and what cannot be done. Make sure the rules are clearly understood and identify all external constraints on actions. State clearly what rules are to be made and what rules will not be made. A game has to be freewheeling enough to allow persons to pursue their hunches. But it will be chaos

without some unifying features that provide continuity.

9. Create the scene, set the stage, instruct the actors, and trust the process. Provide plenty of time for reflection and feedback.

10. Tie the game experience with other educational activities as a part of the whole experience.

The key of successful experiential education lies in adequate content, involving a group in an activity, looking at what happens, and deciding what to do about what has been learned. You will discover that the learning experiences described in this book follow these basic steps.

The leader will learn from his own success and failure, and from the success and failure of others. Begin experiential education with a group that is not afraid to experiment and learn from their failure. These are some other principles to keep in mind.

1. Examine the materials and suggestions in light of the abilities and interests of the group. Define clearly what the experience is trying to teach or what possibilities it has to teach.

2. Analyze the experience according to the degree of complexity. Avoid games or experiences that have very complicated rules and reading matter. Work toward simple rules and materials.

3. Let participants learn by doing. Do not spend so much time explaining rules that there is no time to play.

4. Be aware of people who simply cannot get involved in play. Over 90 percent of the people soon pick up the enthusiastic values of the situation after they get through the initial warm-ups. Some people will just not play. The leader may feel keen disappointment when people will not play, but help these few feel a part of the group by allowing them to be participant-observers.

5. Consider the time and facilities available. Do the methods fit the time and facilities? Are they worth the time and the financial investment involved? Would another method be better than gaming? Do not let experiential training overbalance other methods. Rather, use it as a part of your total learning bag of tools.

PLAY AND GAMES AS LIFE

The Random House Dictionary of the English Language lists seventy-four interpretations of "play." A person can play a flute, play quarterback, play cards, play cowboys, or play spacemen. One can also "play possum," or "play it by ear," or "play with fire," or "make a play for," or "play the stock market," or "play it back." The many uses of this word reveal that *play* is a very significant function of living and imparts a great deal of meaning to our actions.

The many uses of the word imply that we are all "players." As we go through the literature of fun and games we find such words as procedure, strategy, tactic, gain, loss, rules, participants, moves, win, lose, and spirit. But these concepts are true not just of games and play. They are true of life. All human activity includes persons (players) with objectives or goals and resources to gain these objectives. Their rules, customs, and traditions will either limit or assist the achievement of their goals; thus the outcome is not certain and often frustrating. What goes on in a game is somewhere going on in a life.

If all life's activities can be seen in play and games, what is not a game? Things are not games. Objects sitting on a shelf lack human activity and therefore are not games. Production and assembly lines are not games. Preset goals for the many, made by the few, are not games. Predetermined processes and procedures are not games. (They are not much fun either!)

BIBLICAL AFFIRMATIONS

Now we must struggle with theological meanings. If play and games are significant slices of a meaningful life what do they mean to the Christian?

First, play is an attitude of life that magnifies enjoyment and freedom. It is a sense of spirit that turns people to inspiration, bright feelings, spontaneity, laughter, and relaxation in learning situations. It's the way we "feel" about anything we are doing. The Christian lives in a free and confident spirit because he is a child of God. This kind of theology embraces the use of all of life's gifts in all situations. "Instruct those who are rich in this world's goods not to be proud, and not to fix their hopes on so uncertain a thing as money, but upon God, who endows us richly with all things to enjoy. Tell them to do good and to grow rich in noble actions, to be ready to give away and to share, and so acquire a treasure which will form a good foundation for the future. Thus they will grasp the life which is life indeed" (I Tim. 6:17-19 NEB). The activities suggested in this book are invitations to enjoy all that life has in store for us. It is best characterized by a free open-ended spirit, even in the midst of hard work.

Secondly, in the biblical view of life, thought and participation and action are combined in some activities. Biblical language is filled with action language—action verbs and connecting verbs. Physically inactive thought is not to be trusted. It is not "learn it, then do it," but "do it, then learn it." We are to act our way into a new way of thinking, rather than think our way into a new way of acting.

Thirdly, because of the gospel of "a second chance," the Christian is urged to try new behaviors. Old things have passed away. We are in the process of making all things new. But we are often timid and hold back. "Can I really act in a new way?" "I would really like to be that way, but what are the consequences?" "If I could only do those things again knowing what I know now." That's what games, simulations, and learning exercises are for. They give us a chance to test our hunches. They are tentative statements about me, my new life in Jesus Christ, and my life with others. They provide an opportunity to "put on" new ways of living and learn from them, without facing all the consequences of the real situation. Try it on for size! How does it feel? How does it fit your style of life?

This is what Paul is urging the Christians to do in the church at Colossae. "Then put on the garments that suit God's chosen people, his own, his beloved: compassion, kindness, humility, gentleness, patience. Be forbearing with one another, and forgiving, where any of you has cause for complaint: you must forgive as the Lord forgave you. To crown all, there must be love, to bind all together and complete the whole" (Col. 3:12-14 NEB). The experiences in this book are building forms for new behavior. We are responsible for laying out the shape of a new life by constructing new models. In so doing we invite God through Jesus Christ to fill these forms by doing a transforming work in our hearts. "For we are God's handiwork, created in Christ Jesus to devote ourselves to the good deeds for which God has designed us" (Eph. 2:10 NEB).

WHERE TO BEGIN

Work through some of the experiences found in this book. Adapt them to your own situations. Some of them can be done in three to five minutes. Others will take three to four hours. Some can be pulled together for one entire weekend of activities. Do not begin any of the activities until you have the following points clearly in mind.

1. Purpose and goal of the event
2. Group size
3. Time required

4. Materials to be used
5. Physical setting
6. Process

Develop a feel for the game by a "walk through" of the various roles and game activities. Also take notes after each event to facilitate your own learning and to improve the process with other groups.

The resources at the end of the book are suggestions for further involvement in the field of experiential education. If you work through some of the resources and have a group that has fun experimenting, you will discover there is no longer a front of the room and that discovery will change your life!

NOTES

1. J. Bernard Keys, "The Compleat Business Simulation," in *Simulation Gaming News,* March, 1972.
2. Robert Dow, *Learning through Encounter: Experiential Education in the Church* (Valley Forge: Judson Press, 1971), p. 42.
3. E. A. Sovik, "The Role of the Architect in Liturgical Renewal," *Church Architecture: The Shape of Reform* (Washington, D.C.: The Liturgical Conference, 1965), p. 20.
4. Edgar Dale, "The Cone of Experience," *Audiovisual Methods in Teaching,* 3rd Ed., p. 107.

3   DEVELOPING STRATEGIES

Strategy is a concentration of strengths in a series of movements to complete a course of action. The objective is simple—to design a process in which everybody wins!

> *Taking fun*
> *as simply fun*
> *and earnestness*
> *in earnest*
> *shows how thoroughly*
> *thou none*
> *of the two*
> *discernest.*
> *—Piet Hein*

Introduction

Leaders who rely on large numbers of people to get work done spend many hours marshaling their forces. This is especially true in the military and in athletics. Many activities are common to both: forming plans, mapping courses of action, long hours of practice and training, regulating the field of action, critical revision of plans during action, debriefing, evaluation, and restructuring. This process is called strategy.

In both war and games the price is high: many hours of planning, practicing, waging action, adapting, and revising. If those who fight and play are willing to invest such energies, what about those who wage battle in the arena of life? Our commission remains the same: go, teach, preach, make disciples (Matt. 28:19-20). But the strategies are different. There are new movements, new formations, new offenses and defenses.

MAPPING THE STRATEGY

Paul's strategic plan for the church is found in Ephesians 4:12—equipping the saints, the work of ministry, and building up the body of .Christ. These are not separate functions, but relationships that overlap and interact.

In strategic planning the process is a recurring circular model (see illustration). In a dynamic circular process a group is constantly reminded of its central objectives and tasks: personal growth, body-building fellowship, and ministry.

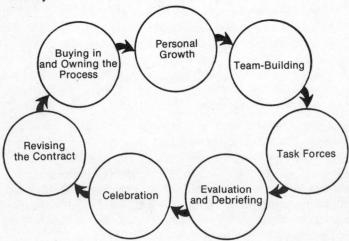

A plan of action for each part of the model follows. Each learning situation is a four-step procedure. The purpose of the procedure is to enable groups to gain specific learnings from their work together. The key to successful group work lies in involving a group in an activity, looking at what happens, and deciding what to do about what they have learned.

Step 1: Explain clearly the goals and purposes of the session. Provide enough content through a short talk or "lecturette." Make sure that persons get the basic direction of the learning situation.

Step 2: Try an activity together.

Step 3: Discuss what happened. In what ways was the activity helpful? In what ways was it not helpful?

Step 4: What have we learned? Do we want to do this again? If so, do we want to do it the same way? How may we make the activity more helpful?

Debriefing is basic, for here most learnings are gained. Debriefing often brings out unfinished feelings and relationships. A simple "Does anyone feel that something is unfinished?" usually will get the group involved. Even if issues or relationships cannot be resolved, the group is helped by recognizing unfinished concerns. The group should evaluate each activity and all activities as a whole. This gives time to resolve and verbalize emerging but unclear insights.

This model may also serve as a basic approach to learning from life. Persons learn from experience. They get caught up in the pressures of life, moving quickly from one activity to another without time for reflection, learning, or appreciation. A learning situation comes from any experience in which one can make a conscious effort to stop the action and ask what happened: Can I identify specifically and concretely what happened in this experience? To whom did it happen and how? When did it happen? What preceded it? What followed? Why did events happen as they did? What activities were most helpful? What activities blocked the process? What hindered progress and development? Who was responsible, and who was irresponsible? Were results satisfying or disappointing?

The power of this approach lies with the individual. Is he willing to learn from these experiences? Faith must be understood in and through experience, which is the loom on which the whole fabric of life is shaped. To be able to reflect on one's experience is to gain new insights and new understandings. When she was admonished to think before she spoke, a little girl said, "How can I know what I think until I hear what I've got to say?" The same applies to our actions. Our beliefs are a result of experience. God works where persons encounter one another so that they become more open and responsive to human need.

One may need to overcome traditional thinking about the length of time group meetings should last. We think nothing of spending four to six hours with friends in meaningless chitchat. Why not spend this time in meaningful learning situations?

Groups must be willing to spend some time together if they want to work effectively. Successful teams spend months practicing together. Commitments to invest time are necessary if a group is to undertake these activities. A three- to six-hour period with one or two breaks provides a good learning situation. Here are some possibilities:

1. Three to six hours on Sunday afternoon.
2. An all-day meeting on Saturday.
3. An overnight retreat.
4. An evening in someone's home, beginning with dinner and continuing for several hours.

BUYING IN AND OWNING THE PROCESS

"Buying in" is an attitudinal process of investing one's energies and abilities in group interaction. There must be a willingness to invest one's life in the lives of others and, at the same time, to own the investments of others. Everyone must be "on board" when the group forms and stay on board for the full trip.

There are several ways of helping persons to see the importance of this attitude. The group should become aware of all the available space in the room. The entire room belongs to all the group. There are no little private corners where one is blocked off from others. Rather, the entire group "owns" the entire space. Space takes on meaning depending on how one fills it! An analogy might be the habitation of an island by a group for a period of time. The group has never been together before in this same way, and it never will be again. This is the group's time and space to use as it wishes.

This activity may be used to help group members understand the meaning of owning space. As persons arrive, they will be placed as far as possible from one another in the available space—the bigger the space, the better. The first four participants are placed in the four corners of the room. As others arrive, they will sit as far as possible from other persons. All room space should be made available for use. An empty room is best, since chairs and other furniture will only be in the way.

The activity begins as a leader asks each person to stake off his own private space. He asks the group to close their eyes and experience separation and distance from others. Group members try to imagine the feelings of other persons who experience isolation and loneliness: prisoners, the aged, the divorced, orphans. They imagine the life of loneliness. They pray for the lonely and for themselves. They ask God to enable persons to move toward one another and toward those who live in the great lonely spaces.

At this point the leader says: "When you have prayed for the lonely, open your eyes and look around. Behold the persons in the group. Look at them as though you have seen them for the first time after a long separation. Study their faces and eyes. Visually survey the group. Turn and behold each person. Try to experience the fact that you belong to these persons."

Now group members will think of another person in the room whom they would like to get to know. Allow them time to reflect on this; then instruct the group members to move toward that person and form pairs. Give each person a work sheet with room to list individual interests, skills, and experiences. Allow time both for persons to work alone and to share the worksheets with their partners. The group is beginning to pool resources for the tasks ahead. After fifteen or twenty minutes move the pairs together, forming groups of four.

Each person introduces his partner to the other three persons, using the work sheet as a guide. Plan fifteen or twenty minutes for this exercise. Then each group of four will join another group, making groups of eight persons. These groups will pool their resources of interests, abilities and experiences. Record pooling of resources on a large sheet of newsprint and place it on a wall near the group. Each group of eight will continue to meet throughout the workshop in the common space they have found.

PERSONAL GROWTH

Growth occurs in environments conducive to growth. Groups can form these environments. Groups are like greenhouses that provide environments for the tiny seeds of new life to be nurtured into full growth. In the small group life of the church, God provided a way for persons to be nurtured in the Christian faith. This is the body life that Paul spoke of where persons are to grow up in full maturity in Christ (Eph. 4).

Persons grow when their personhoods are affirmed and called out. We affirm the personhoods of others in many ways. Here are some exercises a group can use to help build the identity and confidence of each person in the group.

● The groups should number approximately eight persons. Groups stand in a circle, arms outstretched to the middle of the circle. With eyes closed, members will experience the hands of other persons in the group. This should be a nonverbal exercise in which members get in "touch" with the many kinds of hands people have. Some hands are tough and thick; some are tiny and fragile. Some are warm. Some are cold and moist. Some do hard labor. Others do less strenuous kinds of work.

When one person in a group shared his desire to become a surgeon, the group was fascinated by his hands. They spent much time simply looking at and touching the hands of the person who felt that his gifts could be directed toward saving people's lives. Later, the medical student said he felt affirmed in the experience and for the first time became confident that he would someday be able to mend and heal life through his hands.

● The face and eyes are other means by which we affirm the beings of others. As the group stands in a circle, members behold the other persons in the group. In this experience there is much eye-to-eye contact. Each one allows himself to come into the visual presence of his neighbor and presents himself visually. Without speaking, each one simply beholds the other person's being. Bodies and body movements are allowed to speak directly.

● Provide large newsprint and felt-tip pens for each group. Each group sits around the newsprint. With each group member taking turns, have members write their names in large letters on the newsprint. While they are writing, each describes what his name means to him. Each writes the name he wishes to be called. After each one has written his name and reflected on its personal meaning to his identity, the group repeats the name several times in unison. Through this experience the groups have affirmed each person's identity and personhood through three mediums—hand, face, and name.

● Another group exercise, which uses a combination of all three mediums, is an "I am" encounter. One person leads and goes completely around the group. Others participate in each transaction by giving complete attention to it. The leader moves from person to person, placing his hands on the shoulders of each member he encounters, and says: "Your name is _____. You are you, and I am I. My name is _____." Each person in turn then encounters every other member of the group.

Discuss the experience of affirming hands, faces, and names. Let each group member share his feelings and what he feels is happening in the group. What is the group beginning to learn from such experiences?

TEAM-BUILDING

Team-building is a dynamic process in which Christians begin to experience what it is like to be one body in Christ. The need for team-building is discovered when persons experience the unique and indispensable part each plays in accomplishing a common task.

All organisms require care. No responsible person would neglect routine checkups on his body, his automobile, his garden, or his home. No organism runs without proper care. It is important periodically to revitalize the group environment.

Note that teams have to be developed. A group of people working on goals other than their own is not a team. There are two important principles to remember in team-building exercises: (1) you do not have a team until everyone is heard, and (2) do not expect others to be interested in what you want, unless you are willing to take seriously what they want.

Most people grow up with deep conditioning about the value of individual work. Elementary and secondary schools, as well as churches, have learning concepts that teach isolation, competition, and interpersonal conflict. If I win, someone has to lose. Rugged individualism is seen as a strength. The blending of spirits and energies in mutual support is seen as weakness. Nothing destroys the effectiveness of church life more than these attitudes.

Church groups must learn the process of collaboration—getting people together in ways that they can make a significant contribution. This is a process of linking persons with ideas, persons with power and influence, and persons with an intuitive sense of providing care and support. A team is not a group of people who look and think alike. Rather, it is a real conglomeration of people who:

—are good students of the biblical message
—have ideas or specialized knowledge
—know how to stimulate and motivate
—magnify relationships and links to others
—enjoy detailed work
—have authority and influence with the rest of the congregation
—have clarity of perception and the honesty of accurate feedback

The value of team resources over individual resources may need to be illustrated. As you attempt to illustrate the value of team effort in the church, use the following exercise. Provide each person with two sheets of paper and a pencil. Ask persons to work alone for ten minutes. On one sheet of paper have each person list the twelve disciples of Jesus. After each person has worked alone for ten minutes, assign each to a team of six to eight persons. Now ask the teams to work together for ten minutes. Team members compare answers and stimulate one another as a team answer is prepared. Record the scores on both the individual work sheets and team work sheets, and then make comparisons. Score the sheets by giving one point to each correct name listed.

Team-building is concerned with all levels of group interaction. One of the great lessons to be learned from athletics is how winners get all team members involved in the action. This was the strategy of Bill Russell and the Boston Celtics. While other teams seemed to have better players, the Celtics won title after title. The secret of the Celtics' success was finding ways to get all the team members involved in all the action, all the time. No one was standing around. Everyone was involved in the movement of the ball. Sooner or later, someone got free for a good shot. The team was not built around one, two, or even three good players. The strategy came in learning to utilize the best strengths of everyone. This made the Celtics champions.

First Corinthians 12 outlines the full concept of what it means to work as a body:

> For Christ is like a single body with its many limbs and organs, which, many as they are, together make up one body
> . . . .
> A body is not one single organ, but many. Suppose the foot should say, "Because I am not a hand, I do not belong to the body," it does none the less belong to the body. . . . If the body were all eye, how could it hear? If the body were all ear, how could it smell? But, in fact, God appointed each limb and organ to its own place in the body, as he chose. . . .
> But God has combined the various parts of the body, giving

special honour to the humbler parts, so that there might be no sense of division in the body, but that all its organs might feel the same concern for one another. If one organ suffers, they all suffer together. If one flourishes, they all rejoice together (I Cor. 12:12-26 NEB).

"All of you, then, are Christ's body, and each one is a part of it" (I Cor. 12:27 TEV).

The principles of teamwork are not related to team size. In the best sense of the word, a group is a team learning to work together. In a team, all win or all lose together. The principles of team life follow.

The Principles of Team Life

1. Teams are the pooled strengths of a wide range of ideas, abilities, and opinions. Diversity is intentionally sought and is valued for balance and depth.
2. A team has no neutral ground nor is any team member with neutral influence. Each person can either help or hurt the team task.
3. Leadership emerges out of the team's life. Teams operate on the basis of shared leadership. Each person offers leadership in areas where he has competence and insight.
4. Teams arrive at goal definition through mutual negotiations and understandings. Team members tend to carry out decisions that they help make.
5. Teams are built on a high degree of personal investment and commitment. Team life will be characterized by ambivalence, by fluctuating attraction and resistance, by profound satisfactions and deep disappointments.
6. A team should always be seen as a whole. A breakdown in communication at any point directly affects everyone. Therefore, a team moves only as quickly as its slowest member.
7. Each team has surges, plateaus, and declines in growth and development. A team is like other living

organisms—sometimes up and sometimes down. All teams win and lose.

8. Teams must continually deal with both content and process. Content is the handling of facts and subject matter in such a way as to get the job done. Process is the way people take on roles and interact with one another. Whether or not a task gets done is profoundly affected by each team member's ability to interact with other members.

The following exercises are intended to provide team-building influences.

• Standing, the group moves into a circle. An imaginary ball of any size, shape, or substance is tossed into the group. Members can play with it any way they wish. When a member has the ball, it can be any size, shape, or substance that person wants it to be.

After several minutes, develop a group game with the imaginary ball, still playing nonverbally. To be a part of a group that is involved in playing volleyball, basketball, softball, or even bowling without a ball can be a delight. After the experience has gone on for five to ten minutes, the group will discuss what happened. How did they work together, who led, who saw the action as a team project rather than an individual show? The group should pool its learnings from the experience.

• Now the group will pair off and discuss "teams I have belonged to." How did each person work in these teams? What was his place in the group task?

After several minutes of this sharing, each person takes paper and pencil to write a punctuation mark that describes how he feels about the person he has been sharing with and a color that each sees the other reflecting. Then members share the punctuation mark and color with the group, giving necessary explanations. Interpretations should be brief and simple to be effective. After all have shared, ask groups to take this information and come up with a team color and a team name. As another option, each team may develop a "cheer" to be presented before other groups.

● The next group experience is also nonverbal. The group again stands in a circle. The circle represents the rim of a wheel. Each person then moves to a spoke of the wheel leading to the hub. This experience will help members discover where they are as participants in the group. Those who feel they are a part of the group will move up their spoke toward the center of the circle. Those who feel they are "in" but to a lesser degree will put themselves where they feel most comfortable. Those who feel out of the group completely will step back outside the rim of the wheel. Group members test the place they put themselves by moving in and out until they feel comfortable with their position in relation to others in the circle. Then the group "freezes." Each person sees where he is in relationship to other group members, and all see their relationship to the central hub.

Discuss the experience. Usually persons dot the wheel at various points, indicating degrees of participation, leadership, and feelings of belonging or not belonging.

● The next two exercises suggest ways of working together or fighting against one another in a group. Group members stand in a small circle with arms tightly interlocked. With eyes closed, each thinks of a particular spot in the room and focuses all his energies and thoughts on that spot. Then each member tries to take the group to his spot. A struggle follows as each person attempts to move the group in his direction. After a few minutes of struggle, the group should sit down and reflect on the experience.

● The next experience will contrast. The group will move together in a tight circle until there is no space between persons. Group members will attempt to become one body by breathing together and sensing the movement and mood of others in the group. This can best be done with eyes closed and by concentrating on the movements and breathing of other persons. How long did it take to get a sense of oneness with other persons? How do members feel now about the group? What does this experience say about the relationship of the team?

● The group now has some specific tasks to perform. The following materials are needed:

—black and red construction paper, scissors, tape, ruler, glue, stapler, and pencils
—any size round ball
—copies of the church budget
—building materials, such as Tinkertoys, Lego construction blocks, or dominoes

Each group may work on an assigned task, or all may work on the same task. Groups may want to experiment with time limits. Each group gives oral reports, and group members discuss their participation and the processes evident in their interaction. The tasks are these:

1. Make a checkerboard.
2. Devise a game to be played with a round ball. Make up the rules, and then play the game.
3. Pool the pocket change in the group into one fund. Allocate funds to items in the church budget. Work out a consensus.
4. Build something with Tinkertoys, Lego blocks, or similar materials.

Then reflect on what happened. (Do not discuss the project or talk while building.) Who directed the project? How did the group work together? Now plan a project that the group can build together. Develop strategies for building and take time to build without talking. What happened this time?

How did the groups work together in planning, making decisions, and executing plans? How flexible were they?

What feelings do members have about becoming a group? Can group members trust others to make decisions for them? What did members learn about being a team? What feelings did members have as a group moved from one experience to the other? What new learnings will be applied to the next group meeting? How do members feel about the group now?

TASK FORCES

The practice is over. It is time to enter the world of planning and implementing plans with concrete actions. The group should return to their work sheet summaries of interests, skills, and experiences that are listed on newsprint. From these lists will come ideas for specific plans and projects. Now set up a specific group task or project to be accomplished in six or eight weeks that will provide additional material for future long-range planning. The group will need time to reach consensus about a specific goal or project. For additional input on ways of helping groups reach a consensus on goals, see "Consensus Training" (pp. 112-16), and "Developing Covenants" (pp. 116-22).

Each group will need a second work sheet. On this work sheet, groups will fill in assumptions, goals and objectives, strategies, and tactics. The following definitions can be used for items on the work sheet:

1. Assumption—the underlying premise upon which a particular objective and strategy are based. Assumptions are clear statements about the kind of people we are, what we believe in and affirm, and where we are trying to go.
2. Objective—the target or goal toward which a specific action is directed.
3. Strategy—the general course of action selected to achieve the objective.

4. Tactics—the specific steps to be taken to pursue the strategy. Tactics include both names and dates (who will do what by when).

Be specific. Remember, the more specific the plans the more dynamic the process!

Again the sports world may be used to illustrate this planning process. The objective of a team is to score more points than their opponent and win the game. To reach that objective each team has a number of players, a game plan (strategies), and a number of plays (tactics) to score the points needed to win. One major hurdle is the number of unpredictable factors of strength and skill capable of being used by one team against another team. These uncertain factors must be dealt with, for they can determine the outcome of the game. A team must develop a number of assumptions about itself and its opponent. This pregame plan includes assumptions about alternatives available for each team. Once the game is under way, assumptions as well as objectives, strategies, and tactics must be revised. Planning is a continuous process of revising assumptions and employing new objectives, strategies, and tactics.

A written game plan might look something like the following plan:

ASSUMPTIONS

1. Our strengths are speed and quickness. The field will be dry, and this condition favors what we do best.
2. We lack depth at several positions, particularly on defense. We usually tire out during the last quarter. We need to score as quickly as possible in the first half and force the other team to make mistakes.
3. We play well on our home field.
4. In order to keep their defense honest, we will pass more, as well as use more draw plays and screens.
5. We will add four to five new plays to expand our offense. We will need four touchdowns to win.

OBJECTIVE

Score four touchdowns in the first half. Control the ball as much as possible in second half to neutralize lack of depth in defense.

STRATEGY

Use our most explosive plays at the beginning of the game with passes, screens, and end-around runs. Try to set the momentum with our aggressive offense and quick scoring. When we have built up a lead, switch to a basic running game, utilizing the plays that we run best.

TACTICS

This will include a detailed list of plays with specific assignments to players. Plays will attempt to implement the above strategies. For example, Dwight Wagner will do the punting for us in this game, and Ed Wasserman will handle the kickoffs and points after touchdown. Joe Huggins and Jim Ward will return punts and kickoffs.

Look at assumptions, objectives, strategies, and tactics in light of their potential use within the church. Assumptions will include statements about environment, theological bases about God, the world, the church, the ministry of the church, and so forth. Operational assumptions indicate the way an organization will act. This includes who or what group does the planning, how plans are reviewed and acted upon, and how plans are revised in view of what actually happens.

The objective is a clear, simple statement of the target to be reached. It should incorporate the hopes and dreams of all those who helped develop it. The objective is "owned" by each person in the group. The objective should be stated so that it can be measured and actual progress and accomplishment determined. The objective does not attempt to spell out how the goal will be achieved or why. This is done in statements under strategies and tactics. The objective does state what is to be accomplished and by what date.

Once the objective is clearly defined, there may be many ways by which it can be reached. These ways and methods are called strategies. Strategies should include the specific intentions of the group and provide a basis for the way the group works during the next several weeks.

Tactics are specific steps to be taken in order to implement the strategy. They should describe in some detail the proposed action to be taken, the persons involved and their assignments, and the target date when work is to be completed or when regular reports are to be made. Modify plans as you go along.

Let's take a quick look at the total process and see how it's done—with fun!

1. *Assumptions are clarified.* In groups of four to six, persons share their hopes and dreams for the church. They briefly state what they expect from others and what they are willing to contribute. A corporate dream begins to emerge that seems to have priority over other concerns. A priority concern might be to organize small groups for sharing, study, and support.

2. *An achievable goal is written.* Our goal is to organize four small groups for studying and sharing the faith and for providing support to one another. These groups will meet each week from September 15 to December 15.

3. *A strategy is developed.* A planning committee is needed to publicize the program and sign up persons for the four groups.

Four group leaders will need to be recruited and trained.

Groups will decide on times of meeting and materials to be used.

4. *Tactics are specifically defined.* Bruce, Peggy, and Sue will publicize and enlist persons for groups by September 1.

Bill, Linda, and Mic will recruit four group leaders and arrange schedules, rooms, and refreshments by September 1.

The pastor will conduct a three-hour training session for group leaders by September 15.

The planning committee will meet on November 1 and 15 for preliminary evaluations and if necessary, redesign the process.

EVALUATION AND DEBRIEFING

In order to continue to build up the group's ability to work purposefully, evaluation is needed. The purpose of such evaluation is to allow for direct personal expression of feelings about any part of the process, and to get ideas for specific ways to improve the process. Evaluation is divided into three areas: (1) identifying feelings, (2) identifying strengths and weaknesses, (3) providing feedback.

1. *Identifying Feelings.* Each person writes one word on a small card or piece of paper describing his feelings about the meeting. He then turns the paper face down before him.

One at a time each person shows the others what he has written and says what happened in the meeting that caused him to write what he did.

The group discusses this question: Based on what has been said, what specifically will we try to do differently in our next meeting?

2. *Identifying Strengths and Weaknesses.* Group members take another sheet of paper and write paragraphs on the following statements: (1) I feel the strengths of our meeting were . . . (2) I feel the weaknesses of our meeting were . . . Allow several minutes for silent reflection before writing. Then groups will share what they have written. Then the group will discuss this question: Based on what has been said, what specifically will we do differently in our next meeting?

3. *Feedback.* Feedback is a way of giving help and

breaking logjams that tend to block the flow of a group process. Feedback helps members learn how well their behavior matches their intentions.

This group exercise will help in feedback. The group will take time to study each person in the group. Everyone takes a 3-x-5 index card for each other person in the group. (If there are eight persons, each member will have seven cards.) Group members will write the name of a person at the top of each card. Then each member will take whatever time he needs to answer the following questions, using key phrases:

(1) You are most helpful to me when . . .
(2) You are not helpful to me when . . .
(3) Right now I feel (toward you) . . .
(4) Your role in this group seems to be . . .
(5) I have the following concerns about you . . . .

If anyone refuses, this is a signal to the others to eliminate his card. No feedback should be imposed. The leader may say: If anyone prefers not to have feedback, do not work on the cards. This will be a sign to others that you do not want feedback.

After cards have been completed, they are passed to the person whose name is at the top. Everyone should sign his cards. Identification of feedback is important. Time is needed for each one to read his cards carefully. Then he may write on another card a summary of how others see him in light of the questions asked.

Then share. (If someone does not want to share at this point, his wishes should be respected.) Ample time is needed for everyone to respond. In every feedback situation, time should be given for full response and the resolving of feelings.

Any plan that is put into action is generating all kinds of data. Here is the genius of the experiential learning process—learn to plan; plan to learn. Learning from our experience teaches us how to plan more effectively.

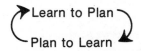

Learn to Plan
Plan to Learn

The following exercises suggest some ways of collecting information and helping people discover what is really going on.

● Give each person a blank sheet of paper and a pencil, and provide the following instructions:

Draw a circle for each person in the group. Assign a name to each circle. Make the circle proportionately larger for those individuals who seem to have greater influence over the way the group does its work. Place the circles in close or distant proximity depending on how closely you feel they are working together. With a solid line connect those people who are working closely with one another. With a dotted line connect those people who communicate less with one another or who are in conflict with one another.

● If you wish to make the drawing of the group's operation more open-ended, simply suggest that each person draw a picture of how it feels to be a part of this working team. The drawings may be simple organizational charts or various kinds of symbolic representations. As persons share, they will interpret the meaning of their symbols. Drawings may reveal the presence of cliques, the flow of communication, locations of cooperation or competition, persons with power and influence, or even what people want and hope for in place of what they now have.

● To further dramatize the nature of interaction, team members might arrange themselves physically in the room according to a person's drawing. This should be done nonverbally until each one is in a position that they feel is an accurate reflection of the drawing. After reflection on this visual image, ask persons to share their ideas about the accurracy of the drawing.

CELEBRATION

Can we design a celebration? No, not this kind. Celebration grows out of a group's life. People receive news concerning victories, defeats, and crisis points. Celebration is persons clarifying, intensifying, and putting into significant form their group life together. Celebration has memory, present life, and hope. It is the act of an organism of living persons who have discovered that not only are they a part of one another, but that together they constitute a body—"Bonded and knit together ... the whole frame grows through the due activity of each part, and builds itself up in love" (Eph. 4:16 NEB). The body is made up of the present and the past to form a pattern for the future.

A celebration begins with the recalling of moments together—the encounters, experiences, and events. Then the group has a clear understanding of what it has to celebrate as they move toward new possibilities and new horizons together.

A celebration does not come from secondhand reading or from what someone else has said. It is a heavy investment of the member's lives and comes from their encounters and experiences together. Celebration is based on the idea that persons who look at one another, touch one another, and talk to one another know how to celebrate together as well. They can share success and failure because they are not afraid of one another. These persons can do natural, spontaneous things and act out their true feelings.

Elements of celebration may be made available to the group. These may be placed on a table if the group wants to use them. The Bible, hymnals, bread, salt, water in a basin, candles, and other elements may be provided.

Silence may make the best beginning. This is not an empty or a nervous silence. Silence can have a deep meaning and feeling. The group waits for something to happen. Memory and hope begin to emerge. Some groups speak quietly together. Other groups are noisy. Often there is a combination of noise and silence. Spontaneity is essential. The group does not need outside help. What to do and when to do it is the decision of the group. Celebration emerges from the depths of group life. Given the time, the space, the elements, and the tools of group life, a group lets it happen.

REVISING THE CONTRACT

If playing games has taught us anything, it has taught us the fragile limitations of planning. Strategy is a process, not the end product. Strategic planning keeps us from the false assumption that now that we have started, everything is going to be great! Only after the teams have been formed and work has begun does the real teaching process begin. We have good news and bad news. The good news is that we know what we want to do and we have practiced it to perfection. The bad news is that it probably won't work!

Those who play games seriously know this is true. On Saturday afternoon a coach goes into a game feeling that his team is prepared. They have a good chance to win if tackles throw the right blocks, if the guards provide the right interference, and if the fullback follows his blockers.

But a coach is realistic. This does not mean that he lacks hope or optimism. But optimism is tempered with tough realism. He knows that chances are that most of the plays will not work. Why? The intangible elements of team spirit, the physical condition of players, the quality of equipment, the condition of the playing field will all be important factors. Not to mention eleven mean guys on the other side of the line! The coach knows that there are a thousand and one forces that can cause the strategy to break down, and he is well prepared to scrap the game plan if it doesn't work.

During the week, the team members have spent a lot of time at the drawing board. They have practiced their strategies to perfection. But they know that charts and plans do not have any special powers. The chart game has to be tested against the life game. The coaching staff knows that everything happening on Saturday afternoon is generating a lot of data for the drawing board on Monday morning. That's the crucial difference in strategic planning. Every present assumption, objective, or policy is brought under critical review each time the team goes out to play. This makes it possible for the team to adapt to future conditions, shift priorities quickly and easily, and revise the game plan each week.

Take a look at the circular process of strategic planning again (p. 36). In it we have a system—the establishment and stabilization of relationships so that work can get done. There is a sharing and trading of expectations about how we will work together. There is commitment to a role and a knowledge of the importance of that role in a team effort. This stability in relationships leads to the possibility that work can get done. When relationships are sufficiently understood, energies can be used for the tasks.

One more dynamic factor needs to be added in order to clearly understand the process. Disruption always occurs. Disruption is inevitable. Only the duration of stable process varies. People change, relationships change, and external forces change. But disruption is not bad. All open systems (teams and persons) are vulnerable to disruption, and this is how change enters the system. New things begin to happen.[1]

As the circular process continues, a different kind of process begins to spin off. It is the disruption process, and it can occur anywhere along the way. It looks like this:

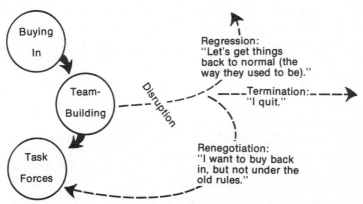

The secret of strategic planning is to know that disruptions are going to happen, to anticipate their occurrence, and to renegotiate expectations in advance. Disruption begins to occur when people begin to feel in a pinch. A pinch occurs when a person feels a loss of freedom or significance and meaning with his role on the team. A pinch comes before a disruption. To keep team life going, people must "learn to tattle when they are pinched." When a person is in a pinch, he must take the responsibility for starting the renegotiating process rather than waiting for someone else to come to his rescue. This revision of contract is necessary to any sustained team effort.

WHAT HOLDS A STRATEGY TOGETHER?

The process begins with a contract. Group members invest their presence, their time, their energies, and their abilities in the process. They play hard; they stick with it. Along the way they find both surprise and static behavior. They experience failure as well as success. People who will not keep contracts cause difficulties and disappointments. If we understand the disruption and renegotiating process, we might hold onto those persons who would otherwise be lost.

However, contract is not the final word. The word "contract" describes an agreement between people, but the word "covenant" adds a different dimension. A contract ends when a partner breaks his promise. In a covenant relationship no condition is put on faithfulness. A covenant is an unconditional commitment to be of service regardless of what other persons do.

Everyone expects good returns on his investments of time and energy. Often this is not the case. We may find that little change has taken place after hours of planning and practicing. But if our fulfillment must come from visible change, we overlook the sovereignty of God and the meaning of covenant. We may hope for success and expect change to take place. But God did not offer us such a contract. He offered a covenant—that we be faithful and never make human success a criterion of our faithfulness to God and to one another.

The cyclical nature of the process demands that we patiently allow it to work, even through rough times. We should not be discouraged by incomplete or shoddy activity. Through continual review of the process, we learn much. Action need not wait on refinement of the process. Groups decide and act long before any process is fully developed. A group can continue to act even when gains are small.

This process does not necessarily produce fruits within three months, six months, or even a year. Five years is a more appropriate span for developing relationships. As the process is developed and refined, its value will be demonstrated a hundredfold. Be patient and be faithful. And try again!

NOTES

1. The idea for this process is from "Planned Renegotiation: A Norm-setting OD Intervention," by John J. Sherwood and John C. Glidewell (Purdue University, 1971).

4 PRACTICING THE TEACHINGS OF JESUS

"This is the reason that I use parables to talk to them: it is because they look, but do not see, and they listen, but do not hear or understand. As for you, how fortunate you are! Your eyes see and your ears hear" (Matt. 13:13, 16 TEV).

Introduction

The popularity of Jesus is extolled in newspapers, magazines, television, and theater, and there has never been a more acceptable time to "praise Jesus." He has become "Superstar," and now we argue about how best to honor him. We can rejoice about some of this change, but there are also hidden dangers. Jesus reminds us of the curse of too much well-speaking. "Woe to you, when all men speak well of you, for so their fathers did to the false prophets" (Luke 6:26). This kind of climate poses a major barrier in understanding his teachings—particularly the tougher ones. He has asked not for honor, but for obedience. And it is difficult to obey what we do not understand.

The following group experiences (or parables) seek to give flesh and blood to some of Jesus' teachings. Many of his teachings do not come easy. They run counter to the accepted way of doing things, and are foreign to our natural instincts. That is why we need practice.

One of the great values of experience-centered training is to aid us in understanding biblical teachings. For biblical habit patterns to take root, they must reach the far recesses of our lives so that the teachings of Jesus become second nature. This takes training and practice. The writer of Hebrews was referring to this in Hebrews 5:13-14.

> For everyone who partakes only of milk is not accustomed to the word of righteousness, for he is a baby, but solid food is for the mature who because of practice have their senses trained to discern good and evil. (Weymouth)

Serious games or "action parables" are ways of trying out new behaviors. Trying out new behaviors begins the process of building new frames and forms that let the Lord know we are serious about trying to live as he taught us.

GIVING AND RECEIVING

"Give to others, and God will give to you" (Luke 6:38 TEV). One of the most dynamic relationships in life is in the interchange (giving and receiving) of gifts. Paul said that the fellowship of faith is built through learning to give and to receive (Phil. 4:15). The following group experiences are designed for groups to experience the power of these dynamic transactions and to learn from them.

The Double Circle

Divide the group (not more than thirty-four persons) into two groups. One group forms an inside circle with backs to the center. The other group makes a circle around the inside circle, facing into the center. Each person lines up with another person, making a double circle.

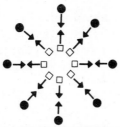

● After the group is in formation, give the following instructions. For thirty minutes we will experience one another visually. Many times a day we see past, around, or through people. Seldom do we visually behold the depth of persons by looking into them. This is a nonverbal exercise of giving to and receiving from other persons for about two minutes. It may be only a visual giving and receiving. It may be a gesture or a touch, or a combination of all of these. The only rule is that it be a natural and spontaneous expression.

After two minutes, the outside circle moves one person to the left and repeats the experience. Continue rotating the outside circle until the circles are back to their original alignment. Emphasize the nonverbal nature of the experience.

● The next group experience continues the double-circle formation. Give the following instructions. For thirty minutes we will share feelings and experiences about giving and receiving. The leader will announce at intervals the following series of two-minute discussion subjects. Each time the subject changes, the person in the inside circle moves to his left one person. In this way persons share some of their feelings with half the group.

1. When has giving been a meaningful experience for you?
2. When has receiving been a meaningful experience for you?
3. Why do you give?

4. What strings are attached to the gifts you give? (What do you expect in return?)
5. Which is most difficult for you—giving or receiving?
6. What are the long-term effects or values of gifts you have given or received?
7. What is something you've always wanted but never received?
8. How do you draw up a Christmas shopping list?
9. What meanings are behind Christmas cards, personal letters, photographs, etc.?
10. What are the best kinds of gifts?
11. What does the meaning of Christmas (God's gift of his Son) say about your gift-giving?
12. What kinds of gifts best nourish the relationships between persons, and between persons and God?

Four Coins in a Pocket

The following exercise will help a group clarify concepts of giving and receiving and will show how these interchanges come alive in small groups.

Each group should have four to eight participants seated in a circle. Ask each group to give a penny, a nickel, a dime, and a quarter to each of its members. The group facilitator should have a number of coins available if group transactions do not result in the correct distribution of coins. Allow five minutes for these transactions.

1. Ask participants to select from the four coins the coin that best fits their own character. The coin is held and the rest are put aside.
2. Participants then share with the group the reason for their selection of a particular coin. Each person will have specific reasons for coin selection related to size, utility, value, inscriptions, or a myriad of other reasons.
3. The participants will then silently choose to give this

part of themselves to another member of the group. It is important that group members not change their choice after making their final decision.

4. Participants will give their coins and what part of themselves they represent to another member of the group.

5. After each gift and reception has been made, the participants will share the personal results of the transactions. What did they begin with? What do they have now? What are the feelings of loss or gain, of acceptance and rejection, of giving and receiving?

6. Participants should now reflect on the total group process. How do you feel? What happened? What was helpful? What was not helpful? What have you learned from the experience that you can use another time? How can you apply what you have learned to the meaning of giving and receiving in the New Testament?

BECOME LAST OF ALL

"So the last will be first, and the first last" (Matt. 20:16). The following group encounters will help persons experience the role of servanthood in the New Testament. Being servant and being last appears in at least eleven different passages in the Synoptic Gospels. Jesus must have thought that it was important. This behavior is difficult to learn. The more we can practice, the more it will become second nature for us. So, let's practice!

Being Servant

● The most profound picture of servanthood in the New Testament is that of Jesus washing the disciples' feet. Here is an example of how Jesus taught by *encounter*.

"If I then, your Lord and Teacher, have washed your feet, you also ought to wash one another's feet. For I have given you an example, that you also should do as I have done to you" (John 13:14-15).

One church, constantly seeking to remind themselves of the servant role, has a basin of water and a towel on a table beside the Lord's table when observing the Lord's Supper. This "fellowship of the towel" is a graphic image of the Christian's role of servant.

If a group is receptive to this kind of experience, the beauty, meaning, and realism of the act is worth the try. Resistances should be talked through and a covenant made to work through the experience as a group. Agreement should be made about method and process with simplicity the rule. A period of teaching about the washing of feet (John 13), and a period of reflection following should be a part of the total experience.

• Another way of imaging servanthood for contemporary man is in the simple act of shining shoes. Shoe polish, shine rags, and brushes are provided for the group. Each group member takes turns cleaning, waxing, and polishing the shoes of other members of the group. This may be a nonverbal experience or open to verbal expression. Trust the group to find its own level of involvement. Laughter is often a way to get comfortable with a new experience and usually subsides as group members search for the deeper meanings of the act.

Provide plenty of time for reflection. How do you feel? What happened? What was helpful? What was not helpful? What did you learn from the experience that you can use another time? How can you apply your learnings to the Christian role of servant?

Being Last

The following group experience is to help persons expand their awareness of each person's influence on the group and the various positions of status, power, and influence in the group.

This is a nonverbal exercise. Have groups of six to eight line their chairs in a row, one for each person in the group. Now take the chair you feel you should occupy according to your influence on the group. The first chair is for the person who carries the most weight in group leadership. The last chair is for the person who feels his word carries the least weight. Test out the chair in which you are sitting and "feel out" your position in the group. If you feel out of place, you may move up or down the row for a few minutes. If you cannot persuade someone to give up a chair or trade chairs, then you may move your chair to the front or back of that person until you find a comfortable place. Then freeze into position. Note the positions of others and then reflect on the experience. How do you feel? What happened? How does the group feel about where other persons placed themselves? How would they have placed persons differently?

The group may repeat the experience to see if any changes occur in ranking.

Phase two of the exercise is a group process of electing a leader. The group is told that they are to elect an effective, fair leader. The group is further told that the voting will be carried out with inverse voting power, in that the group member who ranked last or least influential will have the most votes. (In a group of eight the person who ranked last will have eight votes, and the person who ranked first will have one vote.)

The group is asked to select a leader by casting ballots. Ballots will show the rank or order number of the individual voting, and the name of the individual for whom the ballot is cast.

The group now reflects on the experience. What happened? What meaning does the refocusing of power and status have for the group? What would you change if the experience were done again? How would you relate the experience to the biblical admonition that "the last shall be first"? How would you apply what you have learned to the concept of the Christian as servant?

Implications

Content material may be presented before or after the group experiences. As groups reflect on their experiences many of the following ideas may surface. However, input of some of the biblical material will help groups clarify and expand their interpretation of the experience.

1. "Being servant" and "being last" are primary characteristics of the Christian leader. Those who have assumed these positions have discovered tremendous resources for leading people. Jesus considered the role so important that it appears at least these eleven times in the gospels.
   a. Whoever exalts himself will be humbled, Whoever humbles himself will be exalted. (Matt. 23:12; Luke 14:11; 18:14)
   b. The last will be first, and the first last. (Matt. 20:16; Mark 10:31; Luke 13:30)
   c. If any one would be first, he must be last of all and servant of all. (Mark 9:35; Matt. 20:27)
   d. Whoever would be great among you must be your servant. (Matt. 20:26; 23:11; Mark 10:44)

2. To be first is to receive one's reward now through the predictable outcome of human systems (Luke 6:32-35; Matt. 6:1-6, 16-18). To be last is to become sons of God. The interpersonal transactions of praise and blame, recognition and reward, treatment of friends and enemies, the regulation of credit, and the value of greatness and honor have all been transformed.

3. The worship experiences of the early church were ways of practicing being servant and being last. Both personal and corporate worship emphasized these admonitions. This choice of roles confronted every Christian as he prayed, fasted, or gave alms (Matt. 6:1-6, 16-18). Baptism was a symbol of the readiness to become last (Mark 10:35-45). The willingness to wash one another's feet and to drink from the cup gave Christians a chance to practice the role of being servant.

TWOS AND THREES

"For where two or three come together in my name, I am there with them." (Matt. 18:20 TEV). The following group exercises help persons understand the role of "partners" in the faith. Partnerships seemed to be formed in the New Testament by dyads (twos) or triads (threes). They had several purposes: (1) they were used by Jesus in a strategy of communicating the gospel to a lost world; (2) they were used as a mirror or feedback system to test the accuracy of a person's doctrine or belief; and (3) they were used as a way of dealing with interpersonal conflicts that appeared in the church at various times.

Process

1. Divide all persons into triads (groups of three). If it is impossible to group everyone by threes, have one or two groups of four. Separate the groups as much as possible from one another to avoid the noise from other groups. Participants in each group are to name themselves A, B, and C.
2. Provide each person with a list of the nine scripture passages. Ask each group to divide the scripture passages between them. Each person will have three

scriptures and will make notes on how these scriptures should be interpreted. Bibles should be available for persons to examine surrounding passages. Allow ten to fifteen minutes for personal note-taking.

Scriptures on Twos and Threes

1. I Corinthians 14:29
2. I Timothy 5:19
3. Matthew 18:13-16
4. Matthew 18:19
5. Matthew 18:20
6. Luke 10:1
7. Mark 16:12
8. Luke 12:51-52
9. I Corinthians 14:27

3. After personal note-taking is completed, describe the following exercise. The next forty-five minutes will be a round-robin exercise of speaking, listening, and observing.

Round 1   A speaks   (converses with B) (*10 minutes*)
          B listens   (responds to A)
          C observes   (does not enter into
                        the conversation, but
                        reports his observations)
                                    (*5 minutes*)
Round 2   B speaks   C listens and A observes
                                    (*15 minutes*)
Round 3   C speaks   A listens and B observes
                                    (*15 minutes*)

A. The speaker seeks to help the listener understand what he is trying to say about the scripture giving illustrations and concrete examples. He gives definitions of all words with ambiguous meanings and keeps the discussion on the right track.

B. The listener seeks to understand what the speaker is saying about the scripture. He asks questions and paraphrases back what he is hearing. The listener helps the speaker clarify and expand on his ideas by asking for illustrations and examples. The listener *does not* introduce new ideas.

C. The observer notes the listener's ability to listen. He does not enter into the conversation. He observes whether or not the listener asks questions. Does the listener paraphrase and tell the speaker what he is hearing? Does the listener ask for illustrations, definitions, and examples? The observer reports his findings to the listener.

Interpretation

Allow the group plenty of time to reflect on the experience. What have they learned about themselves? What have they learned about their partners? What strengths do they have as a group? Why did Jesus emphasize the relationship of twos and threes?

Assist the groups in interpreting the experience by bringing out the following points.

1. The Christian is always representative of another. You are not on your own business, but on the Lord's business. Your partners will help you keep this in mind.
2. You are always more than yourself. There are extensions of you in other persons. They live in you, just as you live in them.
3. A brother or sister provides a built-in feedback system to check us on how we are doing.
4. We are never alone. We are always surrounded by clouds of witnesses who have assisted in our growth as a Christian, and even now walk beside us.
5. If we cannot communicate with our brothers and sisters it will be difficult to communicate with nonbelievers. The lines of communication must be kept open between Christians. An unreconciled condition be-

tween persons is a hindrance to the proper worship of God. Whenever estrangement or lack of communication takes place between believers, regardless of who is at fault, both parties are obligated to take the initiative in seeking reconciliation.

6. All human groupings (family, friends) become obsolete if they conflict with Christ's purposes. Opportunities are provided for us to choose new partners in order to be more effective witnesses. Notice that the disciples are called in pairs (Luke 6:13-16).

WALKING TOGETHER

"The light is with you for a little longer. Walk while you have the light . . ." (John 12:35). The purpose of this group experience is to help persons discover new dimensions of relating to one another and to Christ through walking together. Two themes can be developed from this experience: (1) the interrelationship of our lives with all living things, and (2) the way Jesus used the natural environment to teach and to build the fellowship that existed between himself and the disciples.

No environment is better equipped for learning than the one God gave us—the rich abundance of the natural world. The natural surroundings can serve as a symbol of group fellowship and *koinonia*. All persons are different, but there are vital expressions of dependence and interrelatedness. Natural beauty may be a symbol of the social beauty of the group and a vehicle for feelings of group morale and solidarity, which often develop rather quickly in outdoor settings. The beauty of a group assembled in natural surroundings can be illustrated with the following prayer.

Our Father,
There is so much beauty about us—the trees and hills around us.

The surety that the sun will rise and set as always before;
The knowledge that we have found people who share
    some of the thoughts and feelings we share;
The awareness that others came to this beautiful spot
    before we did and gave of themselves, and took from
    this place, and passed it on.
Give us the understanding that we are dependent on all
    living things, just as we are dependent on you, the
    source of all life. Amen.

It is not difficult to see Jesus walking the dusty roads of Galilee when he said, "I am the light of the world; he who follows me will not walk in darkness, but will have the light of life" (John 8:12). The road was his home, and along its way he found the materials to shape his people.

Process

    The group experience should be designed for a period of six to twelve hours. Each group will spend the day together in a natural setting. The purpose of this experience is to grasp the deeper dimensions of our interdependence on one another, the natural environment, and the Christ who walks with us. Begin the hike before daylight, if possible. The early start gives the group the experience of grasping different dimensions of natural life in darkness, predawn, sunrise, and daylight hours. The natural world takes on different hues and nuances at each of these stages.

Suggest that the groups spend two hours of their trip in silence. Each group should select a central place and stay in sight of one another. Prepare mimeographed sheets of scripture passages or other devotional literature and seal the material in envelopes. Each participant will open his envelope at the beginning of the silent period.

Provide each group, six to eight persons, with a backpack or satchel containing the following materials.

1. Canteens or other water containers. If water is not available on the trail, it must be carried in. Some hiking trails have water; however, stream water should be boiled before using.
2. Instant breakfast foods (oatmeal or other cereal), sweet rolls or doughnuts, juice or instant coffee, cream substitute, and sugar.
3. Styrofoam cups and a container to boil water.
4. Hot dogs or canned meat, bread, and fruit for a noon meal.
5. Canned heat (Sterno) if fires cannot be built on the trail, matches, first-aid kit, a few newspapers, and towelettes or a towel.

Emphasize simple, nourishing foods which provide energy. The amount of material that can be carried in a backpack is an important consideration. The themes of giving, receiving, and sharing are basic to the total group experience.

Games While Walking Together

The following individual and group games are suggested at periodic points along the journey. They are designed to help persons explore, discover, and share what they experience of outdoor life.

The Eyes of the Beholder

Suggest the following activities at random and provide time for reflection. Hold your closed fist up against one eye and look through it as you would a microscope. Close eyes tightly, and gradually open them until you can see dimly through your eyelashes. Then gradually open your eyes to full focus. Bend and look at things upside down between your legs, toddler style. Lie down, face up, anywhere that the ground vegetation can surround your head. Explore and probe around your area much as an ant would from its own view. Look forward, then turn your head from side to side and peer out through the vegetation at ground level. Roll over on your back and look up at the canopy above you. Find a real ant and follow him for a while.

Washing Hands

Stop at various places and wash your hands in the soil, leaves, sand, stream water, decaying wood—anything and everything. Wash fronts, backs, sides, palms, fingers, wrists. Feel with the entire hand.

Prickles and Tickles

Divide up into groups of three or four. Have each person find something with prickles and something that tickles. Everyone should keep his discovery a secret until it is time for sharing. Ask persons to sit in a circle with hands in lap, palms up, and eyes closed. Pass objects around the circle, providing time for each person to handle them.

A Wheel

Have the group lie down like spokes of a wheel, heads in the center. Ask them to close their eyes and listen to the various sounds. Try not to identify the sounds, just let them flow into your mind and blend together. Instead of naming the sounds, try to re-create the sounds in your own mind. Let the sounds move you. Then concentrate on the sounds drifting in and fading out like the crescendos and decrescendos of a symphony orchestra.

Color Chain

Take long strips of cardboard or old belts and some glue. Have everyone collect small pieces of leaves, gathering every shade of color possible. Arrange the colors from lightest red to darkest brown on the belt or cardboard and overlap them to form a color chain.

Partners

Divide the group into teams of two. One partner spends several minutes repeating the phrase "I am aware . . ." and filling in the sentence. The other person reminds his partner to stay in the present, by stopping him if he slips out of the "here and now" and helping him concentrate on what's happening right at the moment. Then have the partners switch roles and repeat the exercise.

Budding

Sit in a circle, then turn the circle around so that everyone is facing out rather than in. Become like the petals of a flower or the branches of a tree. Start by pulling in knees and arms and hunching over, all curled up into a tight ball. Slowly open your body to the sunshine, unfold gradually. Shake your heads and loosen your shoulders. Reach out.

Circle of Experiences

At the end of the walk form a circle holding hands. Ask each person to verbalize feelings, observations, or sensory experiences.

Implications

The following concepts about the meaning of walking together can be used either to introduce or to summarize the trip.

1. *The koinonia concept.* Many church covenants have a statement about "walking together in brotherly love." The early church walked together across the Mediterranean world. The seventy walked by two's. Paul and Barnabas, and then, Paul and Silas, walked together.
2. *The pilgrimage concept.* The Christian life is a pilgrimage—a group of people on a road (way) together. It is through walking that we "follow" Jesus.
3. *The presence concept.* Jesus promised not to pull us

or push us, but to walk with us. His first resurrection appearance was with two men "walking" the Emmaus road.

4. *The ministry concept.* Walking together heals, edifies, guides, and sustains. The shepherd walks with his sheep. Jesus taught his disciples as they walked together along the road.

EATING TOGETHER

"Blessed is he who shall eat bread in the kingdom of God" (Luke 14:15). The early church, eager to emphasize fellowship and love, usually preceded the Lord's Supper with a common meal, the love feast or agape feast in which they ate together in fellowship. The occasion was truly a common meal. Each Christian brought a contribution according to his means, such as meat, fish, bread, vegetables, fruits, or drink. The event reached a climax in the breaking of bread and the blessing of the cup, so that the fellowship found its focal point in the redeeming love of Christ. The common meal was indeed a "love feast."

The meal was a potluck experience in which everyone was involved in the preparing, breaking, pouring, eating, and drinking. Informal conversation prevailed: news and views, problems and anxieties, hopes and fears. Acts 2 leads us to believe that they broke bread together, recalled the words of Jesus, read letters from the apostles and other Christians, exchanged ideas, sang, and prayed. Their common meal was like a victory celebration.

Eating together is a sign that persons are free to eat and drink all things and that they are to do so in remembrance of Jesus, who is the giver of food and drink for the sustenance of the body. If we are to practice the teachings of Jesus we should eat and drink together.

Eating together brings out the basic dimensions of interpersonal life. Soft drinks or coffee may be for strangers, acquaintances, co-workers, and family. Meals are for family, close friends, and honored guests. Those we know at meals we also know around the coffee table. The meal expresses a closer friendship. Those we only know at the coffee table we know less intimately. Those persons who have never had a meal in our homes have another threshold of intimacy to cross. The preparing and sharing of food around a table intensifies the meaning of life together.

The recipes suggested offer opportunities for every person to participate in the preparation, pooling, and serving of the food as a total group experience and an act of fellowship.

Recipe for a Common Meal (6 to 8 persons)

1 lb. sirloin steak, sliced paper thin across grain
2 chicken breasts, boned and sliced thin across grain
½ lb. thinly sliced fish fillet
½ lb. small spinach leaves, washed and trimmed of stems
¾ lb. fresh mushrooms, wiped and quartered
2 cups cherry tomatoes
1 bunch green onions, trimmed and cut into 2-inch lengths
1 can water chestnuts, thinly sliced
1 can bean sprouts, drained
1 head of Chinese cabbage, broken into pieces
chicken broth or stock
dash of ground ginger
pungent sweet-sour sauce
soy sauce

Process

1. Provide each group with a large oilcloth, an electric skillet, and paper plates for the various foods. Per-

sons sit on the floor around the electric skillet and foodstuff.

2. Fill electric skillet two-thirds full with chicken broth to which ginger has been added. Cover and bring to boiling point. Adjust heat until broth is bubbling.

3. Each guest puts a few pieces of each food into broth. Do not try to cook too much food in the broth at one time, as the broth must always be bubbling slightly. When food is cooked, each guest spoons some into his bowl of rice which has been prepared in advance. (Sauces may be added if desired.)

4. Add more food to broth immediately after taking cooked food out. This allows more food to cook while group is eating. Many recipes can be used. The idea is to find a recipe that persons can prepare and share as a group.

Recipe for Tempura (6 persons)

Japanese tempura is now enjoyed the world around. It has many components of the common meal with everyone giving, receiving, offering, and taking around the one pot of hot oil.

Assemble an assortment of foods and tempura batter. (See tempura foods listed below.) Each guest spears a piece of food, dips it into batter, drains well and then holds it in hot oil for one to three minutes, or until lightly browned. Drain the oil from the morsel and dip it into the tempura sauce.

• Tempura Batter:

  2 eggs
  1-¾ cups very cold water
  1-¾ cups unsifted flour
  ½ tsp. salt, optional

Beat eggs and water until frothy. Beat in flour until batter is smooth. Refrigerate until used. Place the bowl of batter in crushed ice to keep cool while using. Yield: About 2½ cups batter.

- Tempura Foods:

Raw Shrimp	Shell (leaving tail on), divide, wash, and drain.
Lobster Tails	Shell and cut crosswise into ¼-inch slices.
Lean Beef	Cut sirloin or tenderloin into ½-inch cubes.
Fresh Asparagus	Wash, remove tough ends, and dry. Cut crosswise into 2-inch lengths.
Celery	Wash and dry stalks. Cut crosswise into 2-inch lengths
Carrots	Peel and cut crosswise, on the diagonal, into slices ⅛- to ¼-inch thick.
Green or Wax Beans	String, wash and precook 5 minutes. Drain and cut crosswise, on the diagonal, into 2-inch lengths.
Chinese Parsley and Watercress	Wash, dry, and break into small clusters.
Fresh Chinese Pea Pods,	String, wash, and dry.
Fresh Mushrooms	Wash, dry, and cut medium-size mushrooms into halves.
Green Pepper	Clean and cut in 1-inch squares.
Cauliflower	Clean and break into flowerettes.

Onion	Peel and cut in ½-inch squares.
Eggplant	Remove stems, wash, and dry. Quarter and cut into slices ¼-inch thick.
Sweet Potato	Peel and cut crosswise into slices ¼-inch thick.

● Tempura Sauce:

¾ cup dashi (fish stock) or ¾ cup clam juice	3 tablespoons grated white radish
¼ cup soy sauce	1 teaspoon powdered
¼ cup saké	ginger
½ teaspoon sugar	

Dashi is made from dried fish—clam juice is a good substitute. Mix together the fish stock, soy sauce, sake, and sugar. Divide into small individual serving bowls. Just before serving, place a little radish and ginger in each bowl.

Take This and Divide It Among Yourselves (a table liturgy)

The following worship experience can be developed after a common meal with persons still sitting around the table, or in circles on the floor.

1. The gospel of Luke has several passages that can be used as "table talk." (See Luke 5:29-39; 7:36-50; 9:10-17; 22:14-38.) Select one of these scriptures and read it. Ask persons to share their personal views of the passage.

2. Take bread left over from the meal, break it, and share it with others.

3. Responsive reading:

Leader: Not by bread alone . . .

    All: But by prayer and silence and praise and listening and gratitude and confession.

Leader: Not by bread alone . . .
    All: But by flowers and sunshine and snow and wind in the face and dirt on the hands.
Leader: Not by bread alone . . .
    All: But by words and deeds and work and play and laughter and tears.
Leader: Not by bread alone . . .
    All: But by love and friends and acceptance and forgiveness and talking and touching and sharing.
Leader: Not by bread alone . . .
    All: But by every word that comes from the mouth of God!

4. Music: "They'll Know We Are Christians by Our Love"
5. Unison prayer:

Thank you, Father, That you touch the things of earth and make them new. When the people of God were hungry, you gave them food to eat. When their spirits grew dim, you lit their path before them with hope. So you have shown your kindness to us in the food which we have shared. We thank you, Father, for the bread which gives life, even Jesus Christ our Lord. Amen.

GETTING A CONVICTION

"And when he comes, he will convict the world concerning sin and of righteousness and of judgment" (John 16:8). The purpose of this group exercise is to help your group experience the role of the Holy Spirit as convictor.

The setting is a courtroom with a judge, jury, defendant (or defendants), prosecuting attorney, and witnesses. If your group is small, persons may have to play several roles.

The trial is held in order to get a *conviction* that the

defendant is a Christian. Both the defendant and the prosecuting attorney are trying to convince the judge and jury that the defendant has had an authentic Christian experience.

Process

1. (10 min.) Introduction by judge. The judge introduces the simulation by defining the process of getting a conviction.

• *Testimony.* A testimony is based on the recalling of actual events—not hearsay, secondary evidence, what someone has read about the matter, or what his parents taught him.

• *Confession.* Confession is the direct expression of defendant or witnesses of a personal feeling or action. Describing the feelings or actions of others cannot be considered confession.

• *Witness.* Usefulness as a witness is determined by the nature and degree of his experience with the defendant. Again, only personal observations can be recorded as evidence.

The judge may break into the process at any point if the defendant or witnesses are not keeping within the boundaries of these definitions.

2. (10 min.) Testimony and confession of personal Christian experience by the defendant.

3. (5 min.) Cross-examination by prosecuting attorney.

4. (5 min. each) Evidence of witnesses. (Their relationship to the defendant and their personal observations of his Christian behavior).

5. (10 min.) Jury discusses the evidence and reaches a decision about the authenticity of the defendant's Christian experience. During this time others meet in small groups to evaluate the testimony of the defendant and witnesses.

6. (5 min.) Jury reports their decision and reasons for

making the decision. What convinced the jury that the defendant was or was not, a Christian?

7. (15-30 min.) Evaluation.

Evaluation

The judge leads the evaluation session, relating the simulation to the Holy Spirit as convictor. The following points will help the summary.

1. In a court of law it is one thing to make charges and another to get a conviction. A person does not become a Christian until he is convicted by the Holy Spirit.

2. In John 20:24-29 Thomas is told by ten men, his companions for three years, that they had seen the Lord. Yet, Thomas remained unconvinced. Only after he had experienced fellowship with the risen Christ was he *convicted.* Secondary evidence was not enough.

3. Conviction comes not on eloquence of speech or vastness of knowledge but on reflection of a personal experience.

4. A conviction comes from throwing light on the case. Light is thrown on the case by the evidence of witnesses who testify of things they have seen and heard (Eph. 5:11-13; John 16:8-11).

5. Both evidence and experience are marshaled by the Holy Spirit to convict the world that "God gave us eternal life, and this life is in his Son" (I John 5:11).

5 ADULTS AND CHILDREN TOGETHER

*If a child is to keep alive his inborn sense of
wonder . . . he needs the companionship of at
least one adult who can share it,
rediscovering with him the joy, excitement,
and mystery of the world we live in.*
  –Rachel Carson

*That shift in self awareness . . . implies a
fundamentally new ethical orientation of
adult man's relationship to childhood: to his
own childhood, now behind and within him;
to his own child before him; and to every
man's children around him.*
  –Erik Erikson

Introduction

Nowhere is the spirit of this book more clearly
magnified than in the play of a child. What goes on in this
book goes on in the life of the child all the time. He tries out
roles. He changes roles and invents new ones. He learns
what works and what does not work by winning and losing.
He fashions models of things that he feels to be important,
always experimenting with the possible, attempting to understand it and trying it on for size.

What do children do best? It is certainly not listening!
They play! They talk and sing. They fantasize. They play
roles—cowboys, firemen, cops and robbers, astronauts,
mamas and daddies. They draw and dance and jump and
wrestle and talk some more. Doing is the part of life for

children. Life is a verb, not a noun. Life is action, not concepts. Horace Bushnell, the nineteenth-century prophet of religious education, said it well. "It is to be noted that the most genuine teaching or only genuine teaching, will be that which interprets the truth to the child's feeling by living example. No truth is really taught by words, or interpreted by intellectual and logical methods; truth must be lived into meaning, before it can be truly known. Examples are the only sufficient commentaries."

The games and exercises in this chapter are designed for intergenerational groups—a rich combination of all ages together. The following guidelines will facilitate a more meaningful process.

Take a group of children of different ages and combine them with a similar number of adults. Make sure that some of the children know one another fairly well, that several friendships exist among the group, and that they have come together to do something they want to do. If it is indoors, prepare the room for a party and playing games. Allow for plenty of open space where people can sit on the floor and move around.

Each person should live his own age. The adult does not try to become a child or act childish. Nor does the child attempt to act like an adult. One important principle needs to be remembered. A human being is a person of any age. No matter what our age, we are in our right place at that time and can freely experience what life has to offer at that place in our development.

One of the great values of this type of experience for adults is to help them reawaken their capacity for play. The children know this best and know how to express it. Spontaneous, expressive play in contrast to frantic recreation is a renewing activity for adults. There is no great difference between play of children and play of adults. Both ages need it and use it for a sense of wholeness and mastery.

Be sure to give the experiences time to develop. At first, there will be some hesitation on the part of both children and adults. But all of us have an inner child. The important thing about these experiences is to link the child in each person to the child sides of each generation. Both children and adults are then open to common experiences. As much as possible, let the children be leaders and the adults be followers and evokers of the children's leadership.

To be beneficial for both the child and the adult, the following experiences must be authentic. The children must be able to sense that the experience means something to everyone there. They are quick to detect a condescending mannerism, a look of boredom, a sigh, or a forced smile. They are not asking that adults be other children, but they are thrilled if adults take the time to become a part of their world.

GETTING ACQUAINTED

Set up chairs in units of three. Persons will group in threes for this experience. Adults should make every effort to link up with children. For three or four minutes, each person shares a question with his partners. When the time is up, each person finds another pair of partners. The new trio is given a new question to discuss. This procedure may be repeated several times.

There are many questions that adults and children can share together. Here are some examples, and you can think of others. (1) Tell about the worst thing you ever heard of someone doing on Halloween. Then tell about the worst thing you ever did. (2) Tell about a time when you felt you were being left out of a group. (3) Tell about the first time you felt you loved someone who was not in your family. (4) Talk about a teacher that you really liked. (5) Describe how your life might change if there were no television. (6) Tell some ways in which you will try to be a better parent than your own parents are now. (7) Talk about the money you have to spend on yourself each week—how much do you get, when and how you receive it, and whether you think its a fair amount. (8) Tell about a time when you were deeply misunderstood. (9) Tell about the time you first thought about God. (10) Tell how you think this time could be better used and what you could do about it. (11) Describe your best friend, how you met, and why you like him or her. (12) Tell about Jesus Christ and what he means to your life right now.

MOVING AROUND

Movement will be spontaneous with the children. As the adults follow, there will be initial experiences of awkwardness. Most adults feel some self-consciousness when they are asked to move their bodies, clap their hands, or stamp their feet. This will be a good time to remember how the children must feel when they are transferred into the world of adult activities. Do not be discouraged by initial hesitations. The natural enthusiasms of the children will be contagious and will gradually draw the adults into the variety and festivities of expression. The adults will also have a fear of total chaos. This does not happen. Strangely enough, even quite young children (ages six to eight) have a sense of "what to do next." They know what the limits are, what is appropriate, and what belongs. Trust them!

Touching

For children and adults there are two kinds of lessons to learn concerning touching: (1) lessons in control and (2) lessons in expression. Respecting the "private space" of others is as important as expressing affection. The following activities will provide a sense of involvement and understanding in both kinds of relationships.

Ask both children and adults to find a place to stand in the room where they are all by themselves, not touching anybody else or any piece of furniture. A bell or a whistle can be used as a signal for beginning and ending the game. When the bell rings, everyone is to begin moving about the room, being careful not to bump one another or the furniture. The bell or whistle can also be used to signal two other activities: (1) stop moving and (2) stop talking. The activity can last as long as some intensity of involvement continues.

Children have natural sorts of expressions of affection that adults need to learn. A four-year-old is able to give a firm handshake and look a person directly in the eye. The tender expression of a hug around the neck along with a loud grunt is totally spontaneous with children. The leader might pose the question: If you wanted to show someone you were his friend, how would you do it? If two or three ideas emerge, the group might try them all in a playful atmosphere.

Probably the favorite activity between adults and children is a combination of calisthenics and wrestling. All the adults have to do to initiate this activity is to lie down on the floor. The children then will begin an active bombardment of the adult with handsprings, flip-flops, and tricks. "Do it again" will probably be heard more here than at any other time.

There are many ways that the sense of touch relates to feelings. One of the best ways of helping both children and adults understand this is through the narration of various Peanuts cartoons. For example, Charlie Brown's sister tells him that he will have to wash his hands again before eating because he touched the dog. The phrase "touched the dog" infuriates Snoopy who shows his teeth and takes off after the little girl: "Here comes the bubonic plague! Pet my head and get a handful of germs! Here comes the walking disease-carrier! Beware! Beware! Look out for me

... I'm contaminated.'' Standing on top of a chair, she calls for help as Snoopy walks away frowning: "Touched the dog! Good grief!''

The biblical themes should be told in story form—Jacob wrestling with God (Gen. 32); Jesus and the daughter of Jairus (Luke 8:40-56); and the woman who touched Jesus' garment and was healed (Matt. 9:20-21).

Modeling

Modeling is a way of picturing relationships we have with persons and concepts we have about those persons. Instead of drawing pictures, we use their bodies and our bodies in relationship to one another to build a picture. Divide the groups either by families or by a mixture of families in a group. Limit the size of groups to six or eight. Try to arrange groups in such a way that young children will be with a member of their own family. Make sure that no child is in a group where he does not know anyone. The following experiences can be done either separately by families, or in combination with several families.

(1) Choose a person in the group to "sculpt." Arrange his body in a position that would seem to characterize something about him. Move any part of the body into the position you want and ask the person to freeze. Then ask the group to give your "sculpture" a title. Describe the meaning of the positions you are trying to develop. Several children working on one adult can be a lot of fun.

(2) Ask the group as a whole, to model some animal or object. This will demand some working together. Ideas such as trains, typewriters, or even the inside of a wristwatch can be suggested. It is important that each person feel that he is an important part of the picture the group is building.

Then ask the group to think up something that they would like to model on their own and ask other groups to guess what they are doing.

(3) Pick one person out of each group to be used in a body tracing exercise. Put a large piece of white shelf paper or paper table covering on the floor in the center of the group. Ask the person to lie down on the paper. Give the others in the group crayons and ask them to trace the form of the person onto the paper. You may then want to take the time to cut out the forms, but this is not necessary. Fill in the form both realistically and symbolically with what the groups want to say about the person. Words as well as pictures may be used. After this has been done, the group may talk about what was filled in and add other details. The result may be posted on the walls with masking tape.

(4) Try a "whole body" game such as house painting. Each person begins by reaching out as far as he can to both sides, and front and back. Then he mixes just the right color in an invisible vat of paint which is before him and starts his interior decorating. First, he dips his fingers in and makes hand prints all over the walls and ceiling. Then he dips an elbow in, for large polka dots, followed by his nose, for smaller dots. Now the heavy work begins: stick in one arm, pull it out, shake off excess paint, and with big sweeping gestures paint an entire wall. As a finale, each person holds his nose, takes a high step up and into the paint, then out, to paint the interior with his whole body.

There are countless variations to these activities. Try a tall walk, a short walk, a walk like a penguin, like an old man, on the insides of your feet and then the outsides. Everyone will have ideas. As you discover new possibilities, you will be on common ground, adults and children together, participating in making things up.

BUILD IT UP!

Each group will need a small set of Tinker Toys. It is possible to divide larger sets equally as long as each group has enough materials to work with. Groups should have a mixture of family relationships. No person should be in a group without some member of his family. Groups of five to eight in number work best.

• The task is to build a skyscraper. Each team takes five minutes to plan. They can empty the can of Tinker Toys, but they are not allowed to begin work on their particular structure. Smaller children may be allowed to play with them, but the building of the structure cannot begin. After the planning session, each team places all the pieces back in the can. The leader of the event signals the starting time, and after five minutes he calls time. Let the group talk about how they worked together.

• Another idea is building a bridge. Each team will need a set of Tinker Toys, a number of pipe cleaners, and approximately the same number of participants. The task is to build one bridge after separately constructing each section. Each team works for five minutes on its section of the bridge. Then they have five minutes to bring the various sections of the bridge together.

Divide the Tinker Toys and pipe cleaners equally among the groups.

Allow ten minutes of planning time during which team members will plan how to use everyone in their group. During this time they will also select someone from their group to negotiate periodically with the other teams. It is within this negotiating group that the final plan emerges. When a negotiator returns to his group he explains how their part of the bridge fits into the total pattern. No pieces can be put together during the planning time, but smaller children may be allowed to play with them.

At the end of the planning time pieces are placed in the can, and at the signal the teams have five minutes to build their section of the bridge. Then they have five more minutes to bring all sections of the bridge together.

Is it possible for people who are different to work together? This is the goal of your life together in the church. For a teaching period the leader might contrast the building of the tower of Babel (Gen. 11:1-9) with the building up of the body of Christ (I Cor. 12). While building the tower of Babel the people were confused because they could not communicate with one another. In the building of the church every person works with a central goal in mind—to use his gifts and talents in a loving relationship with other Christians to glorify Jesus Christ.

• Another exercise involves building a mountain. Gather a number of various sized boxes, even as large as 12x12x18 inches from grocery and department stores. Provide the groups with old magazines, crayons, and bright paints with which they will cover the boxes. A stepladder may also be needed. Begin the mountain with a wide base that gradually ascends to a peak at the top. The resulting structure has variety, beauty, and surprise. Groups can spend a long time in a fascinating study of their artwork.

BLOW, WIND, BLOW!

This worship experience is for any number of small groups of six to eight persons. Its purpose is to communicate the meaning of the Holy Spirit in language that all ages can understand and experience. Entitle the worship service "Blow, Wind, Blow," "Let the Wind Blow," or any title of your own choosing. Arrange the music, scriptures, teaching period, and group experiences in order, but work toward some sequence of meaningful movement that reaches a climax. The following are some suggestions that you may add to or supplement as you wish.

Music: "Joshua Fit the Battle of Jericho"
        "We're Gonna Sing When the Spirit Says Sing"
        "Blowin' in the Wind"
        "They'll Know We Are Christians by Our Love"
        "Breathe on Me, Breath of God"

Scripture: Genesis 2:7; Acts 2:1-4

Teaching Period: Small groups can share the meaning of air, wind, and breath. Children understand in concrete ways what these things mean. Give them opportunity to express themselves.

Several points may be brought out.

1. We all know about the wind, although it is invisible.
2. Breath keeps us alive. We must have air to breathe.
3. The Old Testament felt that life was in the breath (Gen. 2:7).
4. The Holy Spirit came as "a mighty rushing wind" (Acts 2).
5. Every breath we take is an act of hope, a choice of life.
6. We never think of breath except when we are threatened with the loss of it.
7. God's people must be concerned about the purity of the air we breathe.

Group Experiences: Use one or more of the following group experiences and provide time for each group to reflect on its meaning.

1. Distribute string and balloons, one to each group. Each person is to blow some of his spirit into the balloon and pass it on to the next person. The last person to get the balloon finishes filling it with air. The balloons are tied and collected in a bunch to be placed at the prominent place in the room.
2. Blowing bubbles can be a part of the experience if you don't mind a little mess. Provide each group with soap bubble materials and fill the room with bubbles. With the help of a guitar or piano teach one of the songs to the groups and sing it during this activity.
3. Pass candles to each person and assign one person in each group to light them and oversee the use of them. Set one candle off on a table by itself. The lights are

all turned out, leaving only candle light. The leader then reads Matthew 5:14-16. At a given signal everyone blows out his candle, leaving the one candle to light the whole room.

4. Draw a large square on the floor similar to the diagram below:

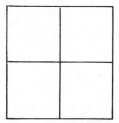

Divide the group into four teams—North, South, East, and West. Scatter an equal number of leaves, cotton balls, or ping-pong balls in each quarter of the square. At a given signal the winds begin to blow. (Everyone blows, no hands allowed.) The goal is to move the objects out of one team's square into another team's square. Set a time limit. The team with the least number of objects in its square wins.

LITTLE PEOPLE, BIG PEOPLE

The following exercise will help both children and adults experience the dynamics of position and size in communication patterns. All of us spend ten to fifteen years being shorter than our parents. Because of this both children and adults see one another out of perspective.

For better communication patterns to develop between children and adults they need to be on eye level, each supported by his own two feet and facing one another. These principles should emerge in the evaluation of the experiences.

Groupings

Divide the group into smaller groups of six or eight persons. The groups should have an even number of people if possible. Make sure that each group has a wide representation of ages and "sizes" of people.

Each group divides into pairs (A and B). Each pair should be different in age and/or size. Give the following instructions and provide time for each experience to develop fully before moving on. Suggest that little or no talking be done during the exercise.

Process

Step 1. One member of the pair should position himself so that he is physically above the other person. Let each pair experiment at first before you make suggestions. Of course, there will be natural differences according to the size of the persons. But you are trying to help them experience what it is like to be on the other end of the scale.

A might sit on a chair, while B sits on the floor.

A might stand on a chair, while B sits on the floor.

The closer B gets to the floor, the better it is.

B might try lying on his back in front of A's chair.

Step 2. An interesting variation is to have both persons face each other on equal levels. Then slowly they increase the vertical distance in stages.

A stands, B sits in chair.

A stands on chair, B sits on floor.

A stands on chair, B lies on floor.

Step 3. Reverse the process. Now B takes the higher positions, and A takes the lower positions.

Step 4. Bring the pairs back into the larger groups of six or eight. The pairs formed in step 1 should remain together. Now each person in the group should position himself in any of the ways previously suggested. All the A's will be above all the B's. Then switch roles. All the B's will be above all the A's. Ask group members to hold each position until each person gets the full visual impact.

Step 5. Spend a few minutes discussing the implications of the experience. How did it feel to be above or below? What were the differences? Did you look at each other or avoid eye contact? Did you feel any different when you tried the same thing as a part of the larger group? When have you had similar feelings in everyday experiences?

6 PLANNING THE FUTURE

"Behold, I make all things new" (Rev. 21:5).

"There is a miracle in every new beginning."
—Hermann Hesse

"Real play is always celebration of life and of living and what life might someday be."
—David Harned

Introduction

The key to "planning" is the maximum involvement of all the people in the project. The depth of involvement will be determined by how the leader views himself as a planner and organizer. Planning enables a church to continually update its program by bringing its current assumptions, policies, and goals under constant review and evaluation. The steps may vary, but some elements are always present: (1) defining the nature and mission of the organization; (2) surveying its needs and concerns; (3) examining assumptions about the future; (4) planning programs; (5) organizing and implementing programs; and (6) evaluation and redirection. Planning will contain all of these elements and should provide maximum participation of the people in each step. The more persons are involved in the formation of plans, the more they will respond to insure their accomplishment.

The most significant aspect of planning is not in reaching a particular goal. The participatory process, in which everyone has a voice as a decision maker is a goal in itself. The ultimate goal of planning is in the personal and corporate growth of the household of faith, rather than in a mechanical following of steps. In this respect, the experience of planning becomes a religious experience.

It is essential that leaders develop skills in planning. This is the purpose for this chapter. It is training in the planning process. In order for a church to plan efficiently and meaningfully, certain skills in planning must be developed.

First of all, church planning demands mutual trust. The relationship between leader and people is a key factor. True ministry involves the feeling of mutuality and of working together as a whole. Proper functioning takes place only when there is true interdependence among the people (I Cor. 12).

Training in communication is the second skill needed for planning and organizing. Goals, objectives, and assumptions must be understood clearly and accepted.

The ability to work with small groups in unstructured situations is a third skill in planning. This is predicated on a basic understanding of group life and process. The local church is made up of many groups operating within the context of the larger group. There is no possibility for growth and change in the church without the supportive influence of its small groups.

The following experiences do not take into account the total planning process. Rather they provide training in planning by developing trusting, open relationships, communication skills, and use of small group process in planning.

The exercises make use of work sheets, simple learning instruments for individual work, and follow-up sharing in larger groups. For best results these work sheets should be mimeographed and given to each participant.

USING THE CHURCH BUDGET
AS A PLANNING DEVICE

The local church budget is a good place to begin in church planning. Lyle Schaller in *Parish Planning* describes the reasons for this.[1]

1. Nearly every congregation depends on an annual budget in the administration of the church.
2. A large group of laymen usually share responsibility in the preparation of a budget.
3. Most church members have some experience in personal budget preparation.
4. The budget is the document that attracts the interest of most church members.
5. The budget can be used as a teaching instrument.

We need to be reminded of some of the hidden meanings behind the church budget. It is probably the clearest picture of what a church does because it includes goals, expectations, and value judgments about the work of the church. First of all, it is a theological document. It identifies the values of the congregation. The budget of the congregation represents its theology and delineates the ministries it develops for personal growth, ministry in the world, and building up the body of Christ. Second, it is a statement of purpose. The listing of priorities in the budget reflects the purposes of the organization, and these are translated into financial terms. Third, it is a box score—that is, it is a record of the winners and some of the losers. What is included in the budget also reveals what is not included. Finally, it is a planning device with specific goals and assumptions. It places a price tag on each goal and includes a built-in strategy (money) for achieving these goals.

● Group Experience No. 1

Divide persons into groups of four to six. Provide each person with Work Sheet # 1.

Take a copy of your church budget and delete all money figures. List the budgetary items and place across from each budgetary item three columns marked I, S, and D. Add other columns for "Budget Now" and "Budget Adjustment." Do not include any budget figures in the work sheet. An example of the way a budget might look is shown in Work Sheet # 1. Be sure to replace these items with *your* church's budgetary items.

WORK SHEET # 1

	I S D	Budget Now	Budget Adjustment
Missions			
Pastoral Ministry			
Educational Ministry			
Sunday School			
Training Ministry			
Missionary Organizations			
Vacation Bible School			
Youth Ministry			
Leadership Training			
Children's Ministry			
Church Library			
Music Ministry			
Recreational Ministry			
Secretarial and Office Ministry			
Building Ministry			
Outreach Ministry			

Consider each budgetary item in the chart and check next to each the ones you would like to see (I) increased, (D) decreased, or (S) remain the same. When you have completed these two exercises, compare your answers with others. Discuss your various values, priorities, and concerns.

Then provide actual budget figures and ask group members to record these figures in the "Budget Now" column. Maintain the total budget figure but in the first three columns redistribute the funds according to your responses. Record these figures in the "Budget Adjustment" column.

● Group Experience No. 2

Your church has been given a gift of twelve thousand dollars to be used in the ministry of the church. The donor of the gift has requested that the money be used only through a consensus of congregational decision-making. The church has gathered to develop priorities and make decisions about how this money is to be distributed. A committee has developed a list of priority needs in the congregation. Each item on the list will take the full twelve thousand dollars. Give this list to each person and ask them to number their first five priorities.

WORK SHEET #2

___ 1. Build a new ramp for elderly people
___ 2. Increase ministers' and staff salary
___ 3. Hire a full-time youth director
___ 4. Begin a coffeehouse for youth
___ 5. Give a special donation for missionary Christmas offering
___ 6. Remodel kitchen facilities
___ 7. Provide new lighting for the sanctuary
___ 8. Open a day-care center for children of working mothers
___ 9. Begin continuing education program for the pastor (a paid year's sabbatical leave and employment of interim)
___10. Develop in-service training for laymen
___11. Replace church's audio-visual equipment
___12. Provide initial investment in starting new mission
___13. Provide funds for a city-wide revival
___14. Begin a ministry of reconciliation between blacks and whites
___15. Provide aid to dependent children in the black community

---

Divide persons into groups of four to six and share results. See if groups can reach consensus on five items. Record group actions on newsprint and display on the wall. Discuss the implications of your work. Are your priority items study-oriented, activity-oriented, object-oriented, or person-oriented? What kinds of items got the money? Why? Did one person dominate the discussion? Do you feel that the money was used in a valid way? What will you do about other items? Would you like to belong to the church now that you have made these decisions?

SCENARIOS OF THE FUTURE

A scenario is a sketch or an outline of our vision without filling in all the details. Developing scenarios helps us to imagine clearly what some of our goals and possibilities are for the future. A future scenario is simply a description of the world, or a small part of it, as we would like it to be at some future date. It communicates our vision by providing views of the future—a future we can imagine real people living in, or symbolic of the kind of world that we would like to live in. The following are some possibilities in developing scenarios. You may wish to use one or a combination of several of these.

● Ask the members of the group to write their own future autobiographies in which they picture themselves five, ten, or twenty years in the future. The question could be posed, "What will I be like five years from now, ten years from now, or twenty years from now?" Ask them to be as specific and concrete as possible. Then, ask members to share with the group.

● Provide a sheet with the following incomplete sentences. Ask group members to complete the sentences.

WORK SHEET #3

Complete the following sentences by writing brief paragraphs.
1. In the future . . .
2. When I get older . . .
3. Someday, I am going to . . .
4. My long-range plan is . . .
5. In about ten years, I am . . .
6. If all goes well, . . .
7. One of these days . . .

● The following are some examples of scenarios. Read some of these to the group to give examples of how scenarios are developed.

Scenario #1

This pilgrimage consists of a long line of people extending perhaps a mile or more down the road. They are not marching in a single-file column, but are clustered in groups of varying sizes. The careful observer notes that this actually is not a pilgrimage of, say four to five hundred individuals, but is really a column composed of perhaps thirty or forty clusters with many people moving back and forth and sharing membership in several different clusters.

This observer also sees that as the pilgrimage moves down the road many people drop out, some for a brief rest on a grassy bank beside the road, others turn off at an intersection and join another column, and quite a few simply seem to disappear. He also observes that as the pilgrimage moves along the pace varies, leadership shifts, and occasionally even the direction changes. He sees this column of pilgrims pause briefly every once in a while to bury a member, or to welcome new pilgrims into the pilgrimage, but the pilgrimage always keeps moving. At times, however, this observer has to set a couple of stakes in the ground to determine in which direction some of the columns are going.

The observer also notes that occasionally one of these columns of pilgrims simply disappears. Ten miles back it was there as a very distinctive separate column. Now it is gone. Some of the familiar faces can be seen in other columns, but many have simply disappeared.

The longer he watches and the more columns of pilgrims this observer sees as they go marching past his vantage point, the more he is impressed by the tremendous variety. He sees columns go by that clearly know where they have been, where they are going, and where they are now. He remembers the definition of the psychologically healthy person as the individual who is linked to the past, is convinced he can influence the future, and is able and happy to live in the present. Perhaps this is also a definition of a healthy column of pilgrims.[2]

Scenario # 2

There is a world out in space which is an exact duplicate of our own. It is populated with men and women like ourselves. They live in countries like our own. They live under various economies and governments, and are divided into different national religious, and racial groups. In fact, they differ from us in only one respect. In each country there is a pathological obsession with human welfare.

As a result, over 60 percent of the national budgets are devoted to a compulsive and hysterical desire for sheltering life from the normal ravages of human existence which we accept more stoically. Billions of dollars are spent by governments on the conquest of disease. Over the years, nations have poured their resources into medical research and today no cancer, kidney ailments, or degenerative disease exists.

Vast sums of money are spent by governments on housing. They have so ordered their fiscal policies that slums and blight are unknown. They are so overprotective of their children that they overpay teachers, and training schools for teachers have to turn candidates away. The perverseness of these conditions reaches its greatest height in their legislation against all private charities in behalf of human welfare. The outlawing of private charity has, of course, stifled the philantropic instincts of the people.

There is only one exception to this restriction against private benevolence. Since the national budgets are so swollen with human betterment appropriations, there is little left for national defense. It therefore becomes necessary for private citizens to raise money for armaments. Thousands of private organizations exist for this purpose alone. There are clubs to buy guns through raffles. People stand with tin cups on street corners to collect coins for the purchase of hand grenades. Drives are conducted to acquire tanks. There are tag days for military aircraft. Cousin clubs sponsor dances to buy uniforms. The national governments simply neglect the problem of defense and let the burden fall on private agencies.

But the inadequacy of this system is apparent to all. People grumble that under such a policy there will never be a war.[3]

Provide each person with a copy of the following work sheet.

WORK SHEET #4

Write your own scenario of the church of the future. Make believe you are living in the year 2000. Describe what is going on in church and what it looks like to you. Express your hopes and dreams for your church.

Ask persons to share their scenarios with others. Suggest that they try to write a group scenario. What plans and actions will make that kind of future a possibility?

LATERAL THINKING

Planning provides for two kinds of thinking—vertical and lateral. Vertical thinking is logical, step-by-step, and sequential. It is based on correct information. Each step along the way is important and builds on the preceding step. Each step has to be correct in order for one to proceed.

Lateral thinking is a technique which deals with a person's feelings as well as his thoughts and ideas. Imagination is the key. Fantasy, dreams, jokes, and play are all part of the lateral-thinking process. A person is encouraged to associate freely, to fantasize, and to dream without risking judgment. Each step is not dependent upon every preceding step.

There are several points to be defined in the lateral-thinking process. Think of digging a hole. Vertical thinking digs the same hole deeper; lateral thinking is concerned with digging a hole in another place. Lateral thinking seeks to get away from the patterns that are already developed and to move forward by reforming the patterns (digging another hole!). Lateral thinking seeks change. There is change for the sake of change. The purpose of lateral thinking is movement—movement from one concept to another and from one way of looking at things to another.

• Lateral thinking recognizes no adequate solution, but it always tries to find a better one. Lateral thinking works with the hope that a better pattern can be developed.

• Vertical thinking says this is the best way of looking at things; this is the right way of looking at things. Lateral thinking says: That might be a good way, but let us try to generate other ways of looking at things; let us change this way of looking at things. Vertical thinking judges what is right and concentrates on it. Lateral thinking seeks alternatives.

• In vertical thinking there is a reason for saying something before it is said. In lateral thinking there may not be a reason for saying something until after it has been said. The young child that says, "How can I know what I am thinking until I say it" is using the lateral-thinking process.

• Vertical thinking concentrates on what is relevant. Lateral thinking welcomes intrusions—happy accidents, jokes, inconsequential ideas— because they can set off new patterns of ideas. In lateral thinking, nothing is irrelevant.

• Vertical thinking moves in the most likely directions. Lateral thinking explores the least likely directions. It seeks to put together information in different kinds of ways.

Consider the role of the court jester in the ancient royal courts. He was to serve as a butt for jokes, as well as amuse and entertain. But to be amusing he had to take an unusual view of life and liven up those things which would otherwise have been routine and dull. No one expected him to be serious, but he was expected to be witty. It is important to remember that the court jester operated at the top level. He had direct access to the king's ears. There were no intervening officials to filter the outrageousness of the jester's way of thinking.

The court jester filled a very important lateral-thinking role. When faced with a situation, the king was able to see it only in terms of his own limited experience. It was the role of the court jester to restructure things in a lateral way, and so provide a different point of view. It is likely that some person in a group should adopt the court jester role, just as people find it useful to adopt the role of devil's advocate from time to time. Once the concept of the court jester's role has been appreciated, the use of lateral thinking becomes possible.

• The following are some activities that will introduce lateral thinking. An important principle to remember is to use small bits of lateral thinking in all planning processes rather than spending hours in a lateral-thinking process. It is better to spend five or ten minutes at the beginning or end of a planning session in lateral thinking rather than to spend hours at a time. Introduce some of these concepts in your planning process at strategic times to generate a new flow of ideas.

WORK SHEET #5

"'And it shall come to pass afterward, that I will pour out my spirit on all flesh; your sons and your daughters shall prophesy, your old men shall dream dreams, and your young men shall see visions. Even upon the menservants and maidservants in those days, I will pour out my spirit'" (Joel 2:28-29).

The Ingredients

Fantasy, like festivity, reveals man's capacity to go beyond the empirical world of the here and now. In it man not only relives and anticipates, he remakes the past and creates wholly new futures. Fantasy is a humus [fertilizer]. Out of it man's ability to invent and innovate grows. Fantasy is the richest source of human creativity. Theologically speaking, it is the image of the creator God in man. Like God, man in fantasy creates whole worlds *ex nihilo,* out of nothing.[4]

The Situation

We have been transported to an area where no human life has existed before. However, the environment is conducive to maximum human growth. The climate and natural resources provide abundance for everyone. We have met together to talk about church. There is no organization or leadership. There is no described place or time for church. There are no resources except the people present (no Bibles, no hymnals, no other resources). There are no built-in limitations in getting resources once the decisions are made as to what is needed.

Work Sheet #5 continued
The Questions

1. What would you like to do? What would you like to offer?
2. What do you see for your life and your church? What should we accomplish together? Where do you fit in? What are your intentions concerning the task?
3. What are your intentions toward others? How would you group? Where? What for? Who would be leaders? Why? What for? What resources do you need?

● Anything is Possible   ● Don't Generalize   ● Be Specific
● Give Examples   ● Be Concrete

● The most traditional form of lateral thinking is brainstorming. Use a large chalkboard or tape several sheets of newsprint together. Write down everything that is said by the group. Do not write in any order. Scrawl all over the pages in different sizes, horizonally, vertically, and upside down. Remember that nothing is rejected or criticized. Everything is written down for later evaluation. The purpose of this is to pile up the alternatives.

● Another group experience might be called idea tennis. It is a mental game, consciously reversing the order of things by avoiding all the rational, obvious approaches and concentrating on all the irrelevant, bizarre approaches. Again use newsprint and a black felt marker and record every statement. The group members act as flints, igniting sparks in other members. Ideas are volleyed back and forth, much like a ball going back and forth over the net.

● Identify yourself personally with any object or person. In other words, become what you are thinking of. Close your eyes and verbalize everything that comes to your mind as you become another person, another object, or another process.

● Use symbolic analogies such as images or pictures to gather unique associations or metaphors. For example, what would a rope be used for if it was stiffened like a metal rod or linked like a bicycle chain.

• Use a fantasy analogy. Anything is possible so long as it can be imagined. The idea is valid regardless of any natural and physical laws.

• Pick a word at random from the dictionary and use it with the problem you are working at. Jot down all the different ideas that come in, bouncing the word against the problem or planning process at hand.

• Consider some everyday situation, object, or activity as if it was the exact opposite of what you thought it to be. Think of snow floating up instead of down, walking on your hands instead of your feet, living on the ceiling instead of the floor, getting up at night and sleeping during the day, putting ice in the stove and cooking in the refrigerator.

And so a few people think you are crazy. It's like two teachers meeting at a party. One teacher walks up to the other and slaps him in the face without any warning. The teacher who was slapped looks startled for a moment, then shrugs his shoulders and says, "That's *his* problem."

These procedures are not a substitute for the hard work of collecting accurate data in planning. But they are often helpful in developing more exciting visions that need to be tested later. One of the most important features of this process is that it tends to free us from past images and experiences. We are so limited by what has happened that everything we plan ends up looking like everything else we have done. The imagination needs more stimulation. This is the purpose of lateral thinking.

Summarize the lateral-thinking process by discussing what is happening. What has changed? Be specific and concrete. Be sure to record the key words or phrases that will capture the intent of imaginations. Let everyone share in building the picture that the imagination has developed. What needs to happen to us as individuals, and as a group, if this is to happen? What skills are needed? What resources are needed? Let the group work on developing ideas and procedures that will enable it to bring some of these things into being.

CONSENSUS-TRAINING

The key to planning in church groups is in giving all the people a role in making decisions. It means valuing people's feelings and reactions, as well as the factual data that is available. Church planning is an open process. The goals are always open-ended. In other words, church leaders do not preset goals and then attempt to bring the people toward them.

The apostle Paul was concerned about the unity of believers. He was firm in the belief that there be no division in the body (I Cor. 12). This expression of oneness is most difficult as groups try to make decisions. But learning to operate as one is at the heart of what it means to fellowship as a body. This was Paul's exhortation in Philippians 2:2-4 (NASB).

> Make my joy complete by being of the same mind, maintaining the same love, united in spirit, intent on one purpose. Do nothing from selfishness or empty conceit, but with humility of mind let each of you regard one another as more important than himself; do not *merely* look out for your own personal interests, but also for the interests of others.

The democratic vote is one of the most reasonable methods to find the opinion of the majority, or the "best" way. But the church's purpose is not to express the opinion of the majority. The church is to express the mind of Christ. The mind of Christ is found in the undivided conviction of his body.

Consensus is the best model for implementing this kind of decision making. It emphasizes both the unity of the group and the goal toward which the group is working.

Persons consider the good of all rather than their own concerns. Consensus also solicits commitment to follow through once the group decision is made.

The following group process is training in consensus. These are experiences in negotiating agreements. A consensus is a shared conviction that a particular decision is the right one. Consensus is a willingness to give up the belief that any one person has the right idea in his own mind. Rather, the right decision is somewhere in our midst. Rather than trying to convince others of our way we seek to discover the direction of the group as a whole. There are certain steps to be taken in achieving consensus, but each group has to work out its own style of reaching and recognizing consensus. The essential steps are:

• Everyone participates fully in discussion of the problem.

• Each member of the group is responsible for stating his ideas and feelings as various factors and possible choices are brought out.

• No one agrees "for the sake of harmony" or to please a friend. If a suggested course of action disturbs a group member, he is to express his viewpoint, his feelings, his reasons. Each person must continually be responsible for putting on the table points of agreement and disagreement.

• When a person honestly feels that he can agree with one or more choices of action (even though they may not be his first choice), he should make this known.

• When all relevant data have been brought out and discussed and everyone in the group is satisfied that a particular decision is the right one, consensus has been reached.

Reaching a consensus takes time. However, this process is much more effective than the others in the long run. Other methods of decision-making may lead to quick decisions, but the implementation of the decision will lag. The execution of a decision depends on the cooperation of every member involved. And cooperation is difficult to achieve when the decision is reached in ways other than consensus.

Before engaging the group in the following exercises, review the process of consensus.

1. Each item must be agreed upon by each member before it becomes a group decision.

2. Not every ranking will meet with everyone's complete approval.

3. Avoid arguing.

4. Avoid changing your mind only to reach agreement or to avoid conflict.

5. Support only solutions with which you are able to agree to some degree.

6. Avoid conflict-reducing techniques such as majority vote, averaging, trading, drawing straws, or throwing dice.

7. Remember that differences of opinion are necessary to consensus outcomes.

WORK SHEET #6

Rank the following items from 1 (high priority) to 5 (low priority). Do your own work, and do not discuss the items with other members. Each person is to work independently during this phase. The experience should not take more than fifteen minutes. Rank no more than five items as number-one priority.

___ 1. We need to provide teachers and leaders with continual training to equip them for ministry.

___ 2. We need to provide teachers and leaders with supervision or evaluation of their work to maintain a good quality of ministry.

___ 3. We need to concentrate on reaching, teaching, and training adults.

___ 4. We need to provide training and resources to equip parents in teaching and guiding their children.

___ 5. We need to assist church members in maintaining close relationships with non-Christians in their respective communities.

___ 6. We need to emphasize church members' involvement in various community groups where they can both serve and come to know others who need Christ.

Work Sheet #6 continued

—— 7. We need to minister to one another, sharing what we are learning from life, and providing a supportive community for others.

—— 8. We need to identify our church with the present struggles for freedom and justice of the oppressed of the earth.

—— 9. We need to abolish all barriers among peoples—whether of race, education, or class.

——10. We need to have each member personally active in daily witnessing to friends and acquaintances.

——11. We need to help each member become personally involved with the Bible and to practice daily Bible study.

——12. We need to help persons cope with consumer and economic pressures that confront them daily.

——13. We need to involve all members in the planning and achieving of our church goals.

——14. We need to concentrate on developing the spiritual gifts and spiritual disciplines of our adult membership.

——15. We need to help people discover enriching experiences for family living.

——16. We need to discover how to make the home the center of teaching and evangelism.

——17. We need to provide ministries for the social needs of our time and our community.

——18. We need to provide more opportunities for developing deep personal relationships with other Christians.

Divide the group into smaller groups of four to six people and give them time to discuss their priorities. Then give them the following group work sheet.

WORK SHEET #7

You are part of an evaluating team selected by the church to determine the number-one priorities and goals of church life. Having reviewed all the data from the work sheets, choose the top priorities under three levels.

First level of priority

1.
2.
3.
4.
5.

Work Sheet #7 continued
Second level of priority
   6.
   7.
   8.
   9.
   10.
Third level of priority
   11.
   12.
   13.
   14.
   15.

Ask the group to place their levels of priority on newsprint and tape them to the wall for other groups to see. Discuss as a total group the priorities of each group. Test for a consensus of priorities of the total group.

DEVELOPING COVENANTS

Persons live out their expectations, hopes, and dreams. In other words, people operate on the basis of their contracts—where they are investing their lives and what they expect from their investments. Most personal relationships are based on these contracts—silent agreements between persons about what they expect from each other.

For planning to be effective, these silent expectations must be articulated and understood A covenant between people makes that possible. A covenant simply spells out in concrete ways what our expectations are and what our intentions are toward those expectations.

Consider the following values of covenants:

1. A covenant makes possible a relationship between people that can be known, understood, and depended on.

2. Through a covenant an appeal can be made by means of the relationship. Agreements may be revised or even

terminated. But a covenant can sustain a relationship. Sometimes that's all we have! Covenants help us get through the inevitable bad times—the resistances, the obstructions, the struggles that make long-term planning processes difficult.

3. Covenants provide a way of testing priorities. Vows made to a wife have priority over vows made to a casual friend. Promises are made to people and programs that we value highly. They prevent us from spending time on trivialities.

4. Covenants ensure repeatable experiences. People who develop lasting relationships have deeper experiences because of the recurring cycles of life together. The common ventures of life become part of a shared experience. Covenants are daily renewals of the same commitments, loyalties, relationships, and satisfactions. They provide the structures that make the repeatable experiences possible.

5. Covenants set limits on the future. In covenants we make promises about the future and set limitations on it in light of the present. We bind some things about the future in order to preserve, in both the present and the future, those things we consider of value. In other words, a covenant is a responsible way of dealing with the future in the present. It limits the future in the light of the convictions that we have in the present. Therefore, covenants are basic to long-range planning and the ability to carry out these plans.

Covenants Provide the Structures for Meeting Human Needs

Consider a basic transaction of everyday life that is common to all. The street vendor offers some apples for sale. He is approached by a potential customer who possesses something to be offered in exchange for the apples. The transaction begins in a tentative manner. The apples are offered. They are inspected, and then they are priced. If there is mutual agreement that a fair exchange is possible, a contract develops; the vendor gives an apple to the purchaser and the purchaser gives the vendor something, probably money. The contract has been initiated and completed. A balance has been struck, and needs have been reciprocally satisfied. Each has gained by the transaction.

This basic social transaction can be carried over to church groups. A church has specific programs, products, and skills that it is offering with expectations of results. It is not dishonest to say that church leaders also have personal needs to be met. This is part of the transaction. The "prospect" approaches the transaction with his own category of needs and expectations. The contract (covenant) develops when there is a mutual exchange of commitments. Needs are met in a reciprocal way. Each party expects something of the other to be delivered over a period of time.

The Needs of Persons

Involving people begins with an understanding of their needs. Persons invest their time and energy in things that bring personal rewards and dividends. In order for you to "contract" for some of a person's investments, that person needs to know what to expect and he needs to feel that he is not being promised more than can be delivered. Sometimes persons will come into groups with expectations that one or two needs will be met. However, the more areas of life that are touched, the more possibilities there are to involve people. An understanding of the many-faceted dimensions of personal needs is basic.

1. The need to enjoy life, to participate in activities that are fun, cooperative, competitive, and playful. People have a need for joy, delight, and ecstatic experience. Life is often renewed and rejuvenated through the spontaneous and free expression of the "child" in one's life. People become involved on the basis of activities that are fun and carefree.

2. The need to create and express oneself. This means doing some original, creative thinking and accepting, and enjoying the new ideas one has and those of others. There are deep satisfactions in joining with the skills of others in creating something new and different. Every gathering of people can be a creative experience. People can be enlisted on the basis of their creative urgings and drives.

3. The need for study, for self-education, and organized reading. This means sharing the world of ideas, having some mind-stretching experiences, and probing some issues of vital concern. People are involved on the basis of their desire to learn.

4. The need to work, the need to be successful in various lines of work in various positions. This includes a need to have good relations with one's co-workers and to develop pride in a work well done. In work, people join with the strength and support of others to share mutual responsibilities and loads. People are involved on the basis of their need to work, which includes not only "church work" but daily work and occupations.

5. The need to give and receive affection, and to be able to feel and express a wide range of emotions. This includes the need to meet people easily, to feel comfortable with people, to talk freely and openly. It means being aware of the needs and feelings of others, and of really listening to what others have to say. It means truly loving people, and not just saying that we love them. People want to be involved at this level—the level of relationships, fellowship, and an expanded world of intimate contacts.

6. The need to experience beauty through worship, music, the natural world, great art, and through the personalities of other people. People are involved on the basis of their need to share the common cup of esthetic experiences.

7. The need for support in times of crisis. Persons need to feel that they belong to a supportive community when

they experience loss, pain, suffering, or death. These are times of heightened awareness when lives are often reordered and changed. People are involved on the basis of the experiences resulting from sharing life's hurts.

8. The need for commitment, expressing a loyalty and devotion to things bigger than oneself. This means being captured by a cause that turns on one's enthusiasm, zeal, and conviction. People are involved on the basis of their need for commitment to a cause.

9. The need to develop and plan short-range and long-range goals and to work toward these goals. This means developing experiences and organizing projects that lead to an exploration and release of one's inner potential. People can be enlisted on the basis of a need to discover their own leadership qualities.

10. The need to feel that one is maturing in one's spiritual pilgrimage. This means following the lordship of Christ in one's life, and in one's own way becoming a new creation. Spiritual needs cannot be separated from other basic needs because they add dimensions of depth and meaning. People are involved on the basis of their spiritual searchings and hungers.

Needs Are the Building Blocks for Covenantal Structures

If a church group is engaging in these many faceted activities they will involve a lot of people. Why? Because they have developed contracts and covenants with people to do certain things. They have agreed to help meet the basic spiritual hungers of persons. They have agreed to help human lives touch an increasing number of areas. What is the basic reason people develop covenants? The answer is—the needs of persons, their hungers and hurts! When you covenant together to meet these needs you are reaching people at meaningful levels. You are using the strength of all the members of the group to help meet the needs of others. The following work sheet is a way of beginning to find the needs of your people. Out of this material you will be able to plan more significantly for the future.

WORK SHEET #8

The following is a list of ten areas where people have basic needs. Check the columns that are appropriate for your own life.

	Needs are met	Needs are unmet	Uncertain
1. Leisure activities (experiences of fun and playful competition)			
2. Creative activities (experiences of creative expression and sharing)			
3. Study activities (experiences in the world of ideas and issues)			
4. Work activities (experiences in projects and common tasks)			
5. Relationship activities (experiences in sharing the emotional and effective life)			
6. Aesthetic activities (experiences in expressing and sharing beauty)			
7. Crisis support (experiences in coping with problems and pain)			
8. Commitment activities (experiences in sharing mutual causes and convictions)			
9. Goal-planning activities (experiences in potential development and problem-solving)			
10. Ultimate concerns (experiences in living one's beliefs in the contemporary world)			

In what areas do you seem to have more urgent needs? Write them below.

What kinds of actions would you suggest for implementing a personal program to meet those needs? What persons do you know who have similar needs? How can you help one another? Jot down your main ideas.

Developing Your Own Personal Covenants

When persons agree to meet one another's needs, they have the beginnings of a covenant. The Old Testament (Covenant) is the story of how a people's needs were met through a binding relationship with God and each other. Biblical covenants have patterns that developed out of the struggles of a people. The design of covenants is revealed in Joshua 24 and Deuteronomy 26-28. The following points are revealed in biblical covenants:

1. Prologue. What persons or powers or groups are making covenants? "I am the Lord your God . . ."
2. The history of the relationship. "I am the one who brought you out of the land of Egypt." Here is what I've done and what you can expect of me.
3. Stipulations and expectations. Here is what I expect from you and how I will tell if you are doing it.
4. Decisions. Do you want to enter into covenant? Is this for you and your people? If so, promise!
5. Provisions, deposit, and reading. Suggestions for keeping the covenant before the people.
6. Witnesses to the covenant. Signatures of those entering the covenant.

7. Blessings and curses. Here is what you can expect to happen if the covenant is followed and if it is not followed.

Provide each person with the following work sheet. Give each person fifteen to twenty minutes to do individual work on the work sheets.

WORK SHEET #9

The following four statements are starting points for developing your own personal covenant. Write out your covenant as thoroughly as possible under each point.

1. Prologue. What has happened to you that you should be writing covenants? Begin your statement, "Since I have . . ." or "Because I have . . ."

2. Expressions of praise. What are your expressions of gratitude and thanksgiving for what has happened to you? Begin your statement, "Thanks be unto God who . . ." or "We thank you, Lord, for . . ."

3. As a result of your testimony and expressions of gratitude what are your intentions (promises) to God? Be as specific as possible. Begin your statement with "Lord, I covenant with you to . . ."

4. Now, state your intentions and promises to the other persons in your group. Begin your statement, "I covenant with others to . . ."

Divide persons into groups for sharing. Ask each group to design statements, under the four points, where there are basic agreements. Share statements with the larger group. Agreements might include (1) statements about meeting needs that come from Work Sheet #8; (2) matters of meeting or assembling together; (3) agreements to encourage, counsel, and admonish one another; (4) undertaking spiritual disciplines together—prayer, Bible study, responsible participation in group life; (5) responsibility for children, youth, and others under admonition and care; (6) finances. Collect the statements for future use in developing a covenant statement of the entire group. Offer cove-

nant statements to church staff with the invitation to develop a church covenant. This church covenant would include expectations and intentions of both people and
church.

THINK AND RETHINK

The following exercise uses the concepts of
cybernetics in gathering ideas from a large group of
people. Cybernetics is a study of how bodies and machines
have similar functions in terms of control and communication systems. In other words, the way our brain and nervous system uses ideas and thought processes is similar to
the same processes in mechanical and electrical systems.

In the exercise or game, the room will simulate a human
brain or a computer in simplified form. In it we will attempt
to manage a network of information and ideas. At the same
time we will keep track of and classify thoughts into
categories. Our thought processes are much like electrical
energy—they are not very helpful unless that energy is
channeled.

1. Ideas are collected from groups of people in a variety
   of configurations.
2. Ideas are organized, and immediate evaluation is begun.
3. Varying ideas are mixed together to form interrela-
   tionships.
4. A continuous change of people's relations generates
   a constant flow of new ideas. When groups are in a
   constant process of change they are less likely to
   become static in generating and gathering ideas.
5. We move away from vested interests—the idea that
   my little niche is more important and has higher priority. Persons grasp the whole picture rather than just a
   part.

6. An educational adventure with complex organisms is experienced.

7. Persons begin to experience a diversity of roles. We occupy multiple positions in life, and we are only partly involved in any single position. But these views and roles connect and interlock.

Design of the Session

1. Classify the priority concerns of the group into four need statements. The four concerns may come from the priority needs found in Work Sheet #6 (pp. 114-15), or from Work Sheet #8 (pp. 121-22).

2. Classify the four need statements as four stations. These four stations may be located in the four corners of a large room. Each station acts as a memory bank that stores the information being collected.

3. Explain to the group that this session is a method of brainstorming ways of implementing four preestablished goals. Share these four goals (need statements) with the group and place them on poster board or newsprint at the appropriate station.

4. Assign a routing card for each participant which shows the participant where he should be (station), and when he should be there (time). Routing cards will be developed from routing tables.

5. Assign a person to each station to record data and to review what has been previously gathered as new persons come to the station. The recorder initiates the discussion but does not remain a discussion leader.

6. By following the routing card each person will work at each of the four stations twice and interact with a larger number of people. The length of time at each station will depend on the amount of time allotted for the total process. Eight-minute periods will take a little over an hour. Fifteen-minute intervals will take about two hours.

7. At eight- to fifteen-minute intervals, half of the per-

sons at each station move to a new station. The remaining half continue the discussion. New members generate fresh ideas. The departing members disperse among the other three stations.[5]

A Room Model

Your room-sized computer will look something like this. Needs or goal statements are taken from Work Sheet #6 (pp. 121-22).

Station A

We need to provide teachers and leaders with continual training to equip them for ministry.

Station B

We need to emphasize church member's involvement in various community groups where they can both serve and come to know others who need Christ.

Provide chairs for twelve persons and a recorder at each station.

Station C

We need to minister to one another, sharing what we are learning from life, and providing a supportive community for others.

Station D

We need to help people discover enriching experiences for family living.

Routing Card

Each participant will have a card that looks like this.

Participant 6

Period	Station	Period	Station
1	C	5	A
2	D	6	B
3	D	7	B
4	A	8	C

Routing Table: 4 Sessions,
8 Periods, and up to 48 Participants

Participant Number

1 2 3 4 5 6 7 8 9 10 11 12 13 14 15 16 17 18 19 20 21 22 23 24

Period	Station
1	A A B B C C D D A A D D B B C C B B C C A A D D
2	A B B C C D D A A D D B B C C A B A C D A C D B
3	B B C C D D A A D D B B C C A A A A D D C C B B
4	B C C D D A A B D B B C C A A D A C D B C D B A
5	C C D D A A B B B B B C C A A D D C C B B D D A A
6	C D D A A B B C B C C A A D D B C D B A D B A C
7	D D A A B B C C C C A A D D B B D D A A B B C C
8	D A A B B C C D C A A D D B B C D B A C B A C D

Participant Number

25 26 27 28 29 30 31 32 33 34 35 36 37 38 39 40 41 42 43 44 45 46 47 48

Period	Station
1	C C B B A A D D D D A A C C B B B B A A D D C C
2	C B B A A D D C D A A C C B B D B D A B D C C A
3	B B A A D D C C A A C C B B D D D D B B C C A A
4	B A A D D C C B A C C B B D D A D C B D C A A B
5	A A D D C C B B C C B B D D A A C C D D A A B B
6	A D D C C B B A C B B D D A A C C A D C A B B D
7	D D C C B B A A B B B D D A A C C A A C C B B D D
8	D C C B B A A D B D D A A C C B A B C A B D D C

NOTES

1. Lyle E. Schaller, *Parish Planning* (Nashville: Abingdon Press, 1971).

2. *Ibid.,* pp. 25-26.

3. Ward L. Kaiser and Charles P. Lutz, *You and the Nation's Priorities: A Handbook for Use with Counterbudget* (New York: Friendship Press, 1971).

4. Harvey Cox, *The Feast of Fools* (Cambridge: Harvard University Press, 1969), p. 59.

5. John T. Hall and Roger A. Dixon, "Cybernetic Sessions: A Technique for Gathering Ideas," *in The 1974 Annual Handbook for Group Facilitators*. J. William Pfeiffer and John E. Jones, pp. 197-202.

7 THE SOUNDS OF NOISY ASSEMBLIES

They are not having fun.
I can't have fun if they don't.
If I get them to have fun, then
I can have fun with them.
Getting them to have fun, is not fun.
It is hard work.
       —R. D. Laing

"Thus it is that men are ever touching
unconsciously the springs of motion in each
other; thus it is that one man without thought
or intention or even a consciousness of the
fact is ever leading some others after him . . .
We overrun the boundaries of our own
personality—we flow together."
       —Horace Bushnell

Introduction

God's purpose for man is to create an environment—persons who are united with him, a body made up of many membranes (members), a temple where God lives through his Spirit. What is God up to? He is building persons who live for him, a body of Christ, an environment.

An environment, in a broader sense, is all the factors in a person's surroundings (soil, temperature, atmosphere, shelter), but in a narrower sense it refers to our relationships. A learning environment includes all the elements that bring persons together in meaningful interaction, and the patterns and experiences that develop from that interaction. People cannot play without an environment. Play brings people to a common place, sets up common rules and boundaries, and provides common aims and purposes.

The question we must continually ask of the environment is, "What is happening?" This question assumes that the setting (person, place, and time) is dynamically and organically put together, and that the setting is generating information, feelings, and experiences every moment. A change in any part of the environment has an effect on every person to various degrees and thereby changes the pattern of the whole. To answer the question "What is happening?" we must become more aware of the whole field of forces at work in the environment and what influence these forces are having on persons.

Some environments are not designed to get a job done. Instead they foster relationships, change attitudes, and develop a commitment to values. Even the task-oriented assignments are done in a playful spirit. An environment based on relationships is a fundamentally different environment. It is a cohesive force because it is based on relationships rather than programs, activities, or services. What happens between persons is more important than how well or how skillfully the task is done. A task-oriented approach will focus on the end product, or the performance. The experiential approach will focus on spirit, affect, relationships, and community. The real reason for participating in activity is not to perform, but to unite with others, and minister to and for one another.

THE CREATION OF SETTINGS

The learning environments in this chapter differ from others in that they involve the movement of larger groups of people. The building blocks of these environmental designs are small groups in the context of larger community. The larger group has a dynamic effect that is impossible for a smaller group. The larger community provides stimulation, expanded resources, and a breadth of wisdom and knowledge that the smaller group does not have. Persons in a small group begin to perceive they are cells within larger bodies.

A great deal of thought needs to be put into the creation of settings for large masses of persons. The setting must allow persons to be participants rather than spectators. Christians are a gathering people. Pageantry and festivity are a part of our heritage. But we have replaced some of the more dynamic aspects of live settings with long, drawn-out speeches, sermons, and meaningless browsing.

People are hungry to participate. The success of entertainment ventures such as Six Flags, Disneyworld, and Opryland give evidence of the need for experience, as millions of people have shown by passing through these turnstiles each day in search of adventure. But plastic technology leaves us a little deflated. No life has been significantly touched. We go away wanting more, expecting more.

Many of our gatherings are like the Platte River—a mile wide and an inch deep. The problem of settings touches all of the educational processes. In a sense, all religious education problems are environmental problems. Can we design environments that are open systems of communication where people can really be in touch with one another and with their true feelings? Is it possible for larger groups of people to initiate and participate in a deeply moving experience?

The following design involved about five thousand people in an interesting environment at Church: the Sunday Night Place Spectacular at Tarrant County Convention Center, Fort Worth, Texas, on March 21-23, 1974. The designers worked toward a sense of wholeness, a balance that would hold the activities together with simple lines and color design.

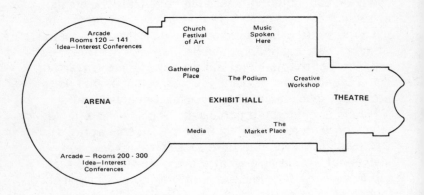

"The Place" was designed in seven huge learning modules that could involve several hundred people at one time in small groups with face-to-face encounters.

The Place

A conglomeration of ideas, information, thoughts, and actions, were incorporated into this unique setting called "The Place." It included:

1. Church Festival of Arts
   (a hodgepodge of show and tell experiences)

How to Have a Church Festival of Arts
Interpreting Religious Art
The Drama Box: Experiences in Using
  Drama in Groups
Photography
Creative Writing
Children's Art
Mighty River Handcrafters
Artists at Work

2. Creative Workshops
  (a potpourri of learn-and-do activities)
  Making and Using Banners
  Making and Using Graphics
  Making and Using Christian Symbols
  The Game Box: How to Use Games in Groups
  Puppet Performances
  Using Puppets in Your Church
  Ministry Through Recreation

3. Gathering Place
  (a combination of sharing, telling, coffee, conversation, and problem-solving)

4. Music Spoken Here
  (a blend of tunes and techniques)

5. Media Center
  (a composite of sight and sound events)
  The Media Box: Communicating through Media
  The Church Media Center Model
  Film Previews
  Ventures in Video

6. Podium
  (a medley of sing and celebrate)

7. Market Place
  (a collection of browse and buy)

BODY SPACE

The environment in which a group gathers is often impersonal because persons fail to see all its possibilities. Assumptions are made about the way space is used and how people are located in that space. The following group experiences reshape the available space and provide multiple opportunities for persons to see each other in a variety of settings.

Clear the room of all furniture. For a group of one hundred or more, a gymnasium is probably needed. For a group of less than a hundred, an average size church fellowship hall will probably be adequate.

Begin the experience by describing a variation of "tag" or "you're it." Have one to five people preassigned to be "it." Explain that when you are tagged you become part of the "it" crowd. Each person tries to keep from being tagged as long as possible. As the game progresses there will be more and more "its." Begin the game with the preassigned "its" going after the others.

After two or three minutes, reduce the space by half. Have the group continue to play "it" in the half space still available to them. Reduce the area again by half and continue the tagging process. The object is to get everyone tagged and on the "you're it" side. Since everyone is "it," everyone participates.

While the group rests from this experience, introduce a new development. Remind the group of how they feel in a sea of strange faces on a busy city street. Persons move silently past one another, preoccupied with their own thoughts, with no recognition or affirmation of another's being. This is the dilemma of masses of people. Explain that the following experience will be a nonverbal way of developing awareness of places and people. Explain that it is important to follow the directions of the leader and enter into the experience without talking (as if you were in a busy airport terminal without knowing anyone). The leader guides the experience by speaking slowly and pausing long enough for persons to act out the narration. Moving too quickly through the experience will reduce its effectiveness.

Leader: Move slowly and silently through the room as you would in a busy impersonal environment where you do not know anyone. Visualize fully the space and the people. Notice things about the space you would otherwise take for granted. Reach up and feel some of this space. Experience this space. Imagine this space is immensely valuable, as if you had just discovered something of great importance. Touch the walls and the floors. Feel temperature and texture.

Still, without talking, observe the people that slowly move past you. Who are they? What brings them to this place? How will they influence your life? What meaning do they have for your life? As you pass someone you know, recognize them in some way without speaking. Still without speaking, introduce yourself to a person you do not know. Continue to move slowly through the entire space. Observe how fast you are walking and how you feel. Now, when I say stop, immediately freeze in your tracks . . . Stop! Close your eyes and reflect on the last experience. Acknowledge your separation and isolation from others. Feel the distance. Think of people who are lonely and not in touch with others. Breathe a silent prayer for prisoners, the alienated, the orphans, and those separated from their families and friends. Pray silently. (Pause.) Now open your eyes and look around, but do not move your feet. Imagine that your feet are bolted to the floor. Visualize the people around you, as if you were seeing them for the first time after a long separation. Remember, you cannot move your feet. Now reach out for the nearest person. Try hard to touch him without moving your feet. Stretch . . . try to reach another hand. If you can reach someone, clasp hands with them; if not, experience the feeling of not being able to make contact. Now put your hands slowly down to your sides and reflect silently on the meaning of the experience.

Ask people to sit down in groups of four to six right where they are. After everyone is seated read,

But now in Christ Jesus you who once were far off have been brought near in the blood of Christ. For he is our peace, who has made us both one, and has broken down the dividing wall of hostility . . . that he might create in himself one new man in place of the two, so making peace, and might reconcile us both to God in one body through the cross, thereby bringing the hostility to an end (Eph. 2:13-16).

Ask the groups now to share their reflections on the meaning of the experience.

DESIGNING A CONFERENCE
AS A LEARNING ENVIRONMENT

Many of us spend an enormous amount of time in meetings. The complexity of organizational life demands a planning process where persons at various levels talk through objectives, procedures, and strategies. Entire work days are often spent in conferences. All of us at various times during a year will invest time and money into groups as small as six to eight persons or mass meetings numbering in the thousands. For all the time, money, and effort invested in conferences the rewards should be many and meaningful. Such is not the case. We find ourselves in a confused environment that offers a mixture of prizes, a bombardment of audio-visual material, expensive pack-ages, dancing girls, and lavish, elegant food. We discover that we've spent five days away from friends and family for a sensory overload of noise, a suitcase full of promotional brochures, and five extra pounds around the middle.

Conference design is an art. A conference can be an artistically planned mosaic pattern or a hodgepodge of broken fragments. Ideally a conference is an organism, a helpful moving sequence of activities that has interrelatedness and flow.

People that come to conferences usually fall into two categories. First, there are those who insist on a leader-centered, step-by-step, programmed approach. They are looking for "the" answer and they expect the leader to offer it. They are not too interested in people and processes. "Just give me the stuff," they say. A well-planned developing process will usually get the response "You could've told us that in three minutes." They expect a highly-structured conference that has every moment programmed. Breaks, dinners, and entertainment are only relevant as a relief from the monotony. You may have a part on the program from 8:30 A.M. to 8:41 A.M.—no more, no less.

Other people are interested in process and discovery. They are not prone to listen to lectures or take notes. All kinds of interaction are encouraged in order to help them discover things and people for themselves. Conference design is an open process. The pattern of the conference is emerging rather than preconceived and preplanned. The nature of this book appeals to this "second kind of person" in a conference, because the person who is expecting steps 1, 2, and 3 is difficult to involve in environmental design. However, if you keep in mind that both kinds of people are in attendance, a workable balance might be developed.

The Jerusalem Conference: A Model of Environmental Design

The conference at Jerusalem in Acts 15 is the model. The early church gathered for free, open discussion and worked toward unanimous agreement (consensus).

The programming was open-ended with mutual commitments to resolve differences. The issues were basic to the development of the early church, for they were to state the conditions of salvation and fellowship. The conference ended with everyone sharing the benefits and rewards, and providing mutual support, trust, and stimulation to others. This pattern is set in Acts 1:15-26. Paul brought questions to the brethren, and after discussion the assembly put forward the decision. In Acts 5:12, decisions were made "by common consent."

Note the orderly, open process of the Jerusalem Conference.

1. No decisions were made independent of the total body. The brethren in Antioch would meet with the apostles and elders in Jerusalem and together they would hammer out a decision. They were bound together not in theory but in reality. (Acts 15:2)
2. The first session is composed of an enthusiastic welcome and a sharing of personal experience. This was not something just "tacked on," but a basic part of the conference design. This relaxed familiarity with each other set the mood for the rest of the conference. (Acts 15:4)
3. The contract and expectations of the conference surface immediately. Each side openly discusses agendas, and lively debate follows. The Phillips translation describes this session as an "exhaustive inquiry" with everyone having full say. (Acts 15:5-7a)
4. Additional input and testimony is provided by Peter, Barnabas, and Paul in plenary sessions. These "sermonettes" are a recounting of personal experience rather than propositional abstract statements. The assembly takes a stance of silent, active listening and they kept on listening until the reports were fully understood. (Acts 15:7b-12)

5. James offers the trial balloon for consensus by laying a proposition before the assembly which embodied the results of the discussion. Note that the resolution is formulated only after a lengthy process of open discussion, additional input, and feedback. (Acts 15:13-21)
6. The whole church (apparently thousands) sought for unanimous agreement and got it! The resolution is passed in a plenary gathering. Also there is full unanimity in choosing a committee and designing a letter accrediting the committee. The opposition dropped objections and were able to join in the consensus. (Acts 15:23-29)
7. With the "back home" planning completed the committee is commissioned and sent on their mission. The commissioning is as much a part of the total conference design as the welcoming is. (Acts 15:30)

The objective for the conference is found in Acts 15:28—the unity of the church takes precedence over matters of majority rule. This principle of conference design and objective is clearly stated in 1 Corinthians 1:10 and Philippians 2:12-14. In the Jerusalem conference there was an early willingness to know and to be known, to let feelings be expressed, to explore hearing and listening, to discover how others were reacting and to attempt new ways of behaving.

Steps in Conference Design

The following steps are a part of experience-centered conference design. Each part builds on the preceding part in a fluid, sequential progression.

1. Get on board and get acquainted.
   In getting on board and getting acquainted, we invest our lives and "own" the investments of others. We

assume active rather than passive participation. We accept responsibility for our own learning and open ourselves to the influence of others. This getting-acquainted process develops a relaxed, secure, unsuspicious atmosphere. We are able to approach others without hesitation and look to others for learning, motivation, and feedback. This comfortable familiarity with one another is basic.

2. Develop the contract.

The contract is made up of the goals and expectations of leaders and participants. It is at the point of developing the contract that the leader sets the tone of the environment. Why are we here? What will need to happen so that we do not go away disappointed? The leader takes an attentive position toward others because he assumes that there will be valuable information from the participants. He releases their power in the group. The leader must establish quickly that he is not selling an idea, solution, or an approach. Rather, he is to release the expertise of the group and help the group ascertain its best findings. He encourages sharing and openness. He does not avoid conflict but uses it to help resolve issues.

3. Introduce the environment.

The environment is made up of people, facilities, learning tools and instruments, and the timing and sequencing of events. The environment is a cultural island, free from outside interruptions, that focuses and concentrates on people's relationships to each other over a given period of time. Nothing is nailed down. Persons, furniture, events, and time allotments are movable and flexible.

4. Help persons become aware of sequence and process. Early in the conference persons should become aware that conferences are not put together in random ways. Rather, each event builds on the one be-

fore and penetrates the one following. The ball begins to roll. The whole movement has balance. Even meals and recreation have significant parts to play in the total process.

It is important to remember that the design should be modified while in progress. This is a matter of redirecting the movement after getting data on needs and expectations. Leadership must continually ask, "What designs best achieve the objectives of the conference?" and "What has happened to give us data to direct the conference in different ways?" Again, this type of conference is not a first, second, or third step-by-step procedure that must be followed. It is a process of collecting information while defining the problem, considering alternatives, and implementing action. The planning process is dynamic and continues during the conference. Protocol, specific rules of order, and majority rule are of little consequence in experiential conference design.

5. Identify and experience the feedback system.

All along the way persons must become aware of and explore the experiences that are emerging, and integrate these processes into personal and corporate behavior. Feedback constantly asks the question—, "What is happening to you as a person?" and "What is happening to us as a group?" These times must be planned for and integrated into the total process. *Feedback and evaluation are related to participants rather than to program.* What has happened to you? What have you experienced? What have you learned that you can use tomorrow, next week, next year, or for a lifetime. What did the environment contain that caused you to learn? If you were going to do it again what would you change? These questions must be dealt with continually through the conference, rather than in one feedback evaluation at the end.

Remember that the basic foundation of experiential training is processing the data that are being generated by debriefing every experience. If we are training for life as it is "back home" then we must make sure that there are possibilities for the transfer of that training. This comes from talking through each experience. It is allowing sufficient "air time" for experiences to be thoroughly sifted out. The debriefing process is a vital part of the organic sequence of activities. Complete all "unfinished business" at the end of each day.

6. Begin each new day with a summary of what happened previously.

Where have we been, and where are we going? What is emerging, what are the roadblocks, and what is keeping us from going where we want to go?

7. Develop follow-up and closure activities.

Keep in mind what is going to happen after the conference. Will the group be meeting again? Do members have access to one another for further follow-up sessions? What are the developing contracts for back-home application? Goal-setting should be planned early so that reassessment can be made both during the middle and at the end of the conference. Closure is closing the door on the conference and reentering the normal world of activities.

The following design pictures the conference process. For want of a better name they are called "L meetings." The flow and sequence of events moves forward but also loops back into debriefing, evaluating, and redirecting before moving forward again. In both the movement forward and looping back the momentum accelerates toward meaningful celebration and closure.

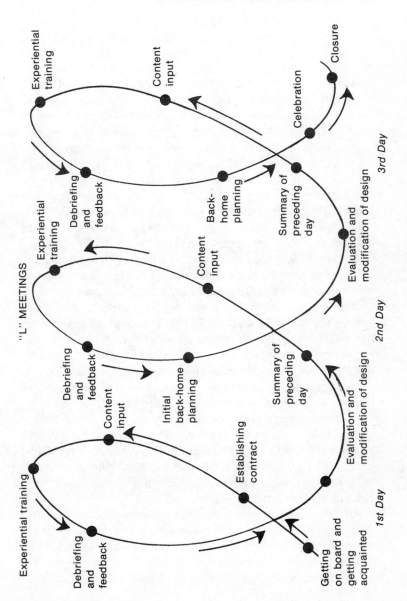

The Building Blocks of Conference Design

The basic building blocks of conference design are small groups. This is a simple structure with no elaborate set-ups that detract from personal communication. Through small groups we get acquainted; experience the movement of conference events; grasp and digest content; plan back home activities; and celebrate our experiences together. This series of small-group events become the basic building blocks of conference design. A small group may range from two to fifteen persons. They assemble for the purpose of generating information, experiencing the learning environment, and trying out new behavior.

Games, simulations, play, and exercises are used to facilitate communication and problem-solving. Leadership, new ideas, successes and failures begin to emerge as persons become more aware of their personal and corporate strengths through debriefing and evaluation.

Content materials are provided by lecturettes, panels, symposiums, and debates. Content is used as a learning map to help persons make sense out of what they are experiencing. Work sheets and newsprint are the basic materials. Work sheets provide opportunities for persons to work alone and in smaller groups. They may be used to facilitate a person's thinking through brief essays, checklists, true/false statements, or ranking scales. Newsprint can be placed on the wall for group summaries and consensus-building in the larger groups. Tinker Toys, Lego construction blocks, marbles, and other "gaming" materials provide another simple, but meaningful way of experiencing the environment.

All materials are simple and inexpensive. Remember that these conferences are designed in order to learn from experience. Anything that detracts from our experiences with one another is inappropriate. Multi-media devices are excellent for some types of conferences, but not this one!

Anything that has to be plugged in to electrical outlets is just excess baggage.

A PATIO CONVERSATION DINNER

The title of this group experience is descriptive of both its origin and its purpose. The model for the dinner was discovered in New Orleans, where entertainment is often on the small patios of homes and apartments. For many people the patio setting denotes charm and leisurely dining. The second word, conversation, provides purpose for the dinner. People are concerned about the quality of their time even if they are "just partying." The search for closeness and shared life seems to suggest that even leisure time be spent in meaningful ways. It is possible to spend four hours in the midst of a large group and never share a single important part of life with another person.

This entertainment model is for large numbers of people, divided into small groups. The dinner is designed for multiples of thirty-two people. Prior to each of the four courses of the meal, the guests change tables. This way each guest will dine with twelve different persons during the evening. The environment that is created will involve the senses of taste, smell, sight, and hearing.

The key to the rotation of tables is in the name tag assignments. Each table is identified by a street intersection. The eight street intersections listed below are only examples of street names. Substitute actual names of streets in your city for each of these. When working with thirty-two persons, eight intersections (sixteen streets) are needed for the eight tables (four persons to a table). To serve sixty-four people, make two sets of intersections using different names for all the streets (for ninety-six people, use three sets, and so on in multiples).

Code Number	Example	Your street names	Code Number
1	Hillsboro and Woodmont =	_____ and _____	1
2	Nolensville and Lafayette =	_____ and _____	2
3	Old Hickory and Gallatin =	_____ and _____	3
4	Belle Meade and Jackson =	_____ and _____	4
5	Charlotte and 40th Avenue =	_____ and _____	5
6	Franklin and Harding Place =	_____ and _____	6
7	Briley Parkway and Murfreesboro =	_____ and _____	7
8	Church Street and 7th Avenue =	_____ and _____	8

Rotation List

After the names of your streets are substituted in the intersection list, the name tags can be made. Guests are given a name tag as soon as they arrive. Below are thirty-two name tag codes. Using your newly devised intersection list, compile your own name tags.

For example, name tag number one calls for the code number "1567." Using the names in our list of examples, we would make out the name tag like this:

Code Number

	Name _____
1	Hillsboro and Woodmont
5	Charlotte and 40th Avenue
6	Franklin and Harding Place
7	Briley Parkway and Murfreesboro

When you make your own cards, you will simply substitute the street names you have chosen.

Thirty-Two Name Tag Codes

1. 1567	9. 8475	17. 4721	25. 6137
2. 1243	10. 4685	18. 1325	26. 6274
3. 2576	11. 1482	19. 2768	27. 3874
4. 7238	12. 2831	20. 7852	28. 5264
5. 8351	13. 7613	21. 3541	29. 6352
6. 4518	14. 8746	22. 5783	30. 6418
7. 2184	15. 4863	23. 3126	31. 3657
8. 7425	16. 8632	24. 5147	32. 5316

Patio Dinner Ideas

The following menus are suggested to stimulate your thinking. Some foods common to the locale of your city or area will give authenticity to the dinner. Each menu consists of four courses.

A Night in Old New Orleans
First Course—Tomato or V-8 juice
      —Serve with snack crackers
Second Course—Green combination salad with dressing
      —Again serve with crackers
Third Course—Shrimp or chicken jambalaya with hard rolls and butter
Fourth Course—French pastry such as petit fours or individual cakes.
      —Serve New Orleans coffee (cafe au lait)

Winter Holiday
First Course—Hot soup, preferably thin soup such as onion or bouillon
      —Serve with crackers or bread sticks
Second Course—Congealed salad
      —Serve with snack crackers
Third Course—Pork chops with dressing and gravy, green beans, cooked apples, hot roll and butter
Fourth Course—Individual pies
      —Have coffee available

General Room Decorations
and Focal Attractions

This dining model allows for creativity in decorating. An outdoor patio will be the easiest setting to decorate so, if space and climate will allow, plan to eat outside. If necessary, pot some small tree limbs and flowers, and bring them to the yard. Place patio lanterns and torches in corners for lighting. The table candlelight will add the remaining quantity of light needed. For background music, use a tape recorder with pretaped dinner music. Decide on one main area of interest and spotlight some extra trees, flowers, or a water fountain. Arrange the card tables and chairs with enough room so that guests may switch tables with ease.

An indoor patio environment can be designed around focal points from the out-of-door settings. For example, the trickle of water falling down cliffs and over stones is simulated in the fiberglass, recycling water fountains sold by furniture and patio shops. In fact, many store owners lend out these display fixtures as a courtesy to customers. Some individuals may have small indoor fountains in their homes. Search out the available sources before beginning to make your own fountain or pool. A small pool may be constructed by using a recycling pump to circulate the water down a pile of stones enclosed in a plastic container, or a concrete yard fountain may be used inside a plastic pool. Surround the pool or fountain with many live trees or potted branches, plus potted plants and artifical flower arrangements. Fill the entire dining area with plants and flowers.

A winter focal point might include a bird bath and artificial Christmas trees. The floor area where the bird bath and trees are placed can be covered with miniature, twinkling Christmas tree lights. White polyester pillow filling (nonflammable materials only) spread thinly over the lights creates the illusion of snowy ground. Artificial snow in pressurized cans may be used on the bird bath. Small artificial birds of red, green, blue, orange, and white give an active feeling to the winter scene. Spotlight the total area with a rotating, tri-colored Christmas tree spot.

Centerpiece and Table Decor

The street intersections are used as the table centerpieces. Neatly letter the street names onto strips of poster board (approximately 2 x 12 inches). Attach the two street names to a 12-inch dowel rod with tape, and insert the rod into a styrofoam base (see sketch). A candle placed in another corner of the base and covered with a hurricane lamp globe provides sufficient lighting. Add green ivy, fresh or artificial flowers to the base for more color. The seating arrangement requires tables that seat four persons to a table. Choose table coverings to blend with the general decoration theme.

A Word about Serving the Tables

Decide to either enlist servers prior to the party, or have someone designated to enlist the servers from among the guests. This choice will depend on the guest list. At parties where guests are more formally dressed it is somewhat awkward to ask the guests to serve one another. However, if you feel you can call on their help, the dining can be heightened and enlivened by having the guests serve as the helpers.

Plan on having at least two servers for each of the eight tables. The food will be served in the preparation area, and the servers will deliver the individual servings to the tables. If the servers are also the guests, they will join their table for the remainder of that particular course. Use different guests to help with each of the four courses. If persons other than guests are asked to help with the serving responsibilities, include a special table and ask them to join in the excitement of being on the host/hostess team. In many instances, the persons who are hosts and hostesses often have a more enjoyable time than anyone else. After all, they are sharing an enjoyable task.

Who Signals When to Rotate?

One person should be in charge of the instruction-giving duties for a patio conversation dinner. This person also guides the guests to a designated area where they obtain name tags and wait until the dinner commences. Brief instructions may be given to the guests when they have all arrived, "The meal consists of four-courses. The name tag will indicate the table to which you are assigned. The first intersection listed on the tag tells you where to sit for the first course, the second intersection indicates your table for the second course, and so on through the evening. The time for you to move from table to table will be announced, and everyone will move at the same time."

The four-course meal can be divided generally into the following approximate time segments: first course (appetizer)—thirty minutes; second course (salad)—forty-five minutes; third course (main dish)—forty-five minutes; and fourth course (dessert)—forty-five minutes, or more. Remember that people are not eating the entire time at each table. They are also encouraged to share in conversation and listen to music. Vary the time segments to fit your own needs.

These suggestions for the patio conversation dinner will give a brief idea of the mechanics involved in preparing for a large group to assemble for food and fellowship. Keep in mind during the planning that you are attempting to furnish an environment for meaningful conversations and experiences. Try to think of each one of your guests individually, if you know them. Think of both their needs and your own needs as you plan to host the party. Enjoy yourself—if you don't enjoy entertaining in this way, don't do it. The rewards of being the servant and host means much to some people. If you are one of these persons, try this model.

A FESTIVAL OF THE SENSES

Creativity is no small matter! Working with our hands draws forth and pulls together the whole experience of an individual. The "Festival of the Senses" is an attempt to experience the creativity of a group of persons. The approach is more than merely viewing works of art. It is designed to be a learning experience as well as an aesthetic, appreciative experience.

Many people, particularly children, have felt the frustration that comes from being in an art museum, or even a store, and looking at an object that cannot be touched. Have you seen a velvet cushion that draws your hand out to stroke its nap? Have you seen a candle that you just had to sniff? Have you smelled an apple pie that makes your mouth water? Have you scanned a sheet of music that you longed to hear played?

Taking a cue from the child who immediately reaches out for the desired object to satisfy his curiosity, this festival model deals with the senses, allowing time and space for experimentation. All five senses are involved: sight, sound, taste, touch, and smell. With this approach to a festival it is necessary to plan carefully in advance so that all five areas will be represented by creative works.

Solicitation of materials will ensure entries for the five categories. As the contributions are brought to the display room(s), they are placed in the most descriptive category. Items for display are encouraged by means of publicity about the festival. Unless a festival is an annual event, there may be hesitancy on the part of many persons about bringing their materials. Via printed publicity and word of mouth, encourage the ideas that we aren't sharing our creations for judgment and criticism, but as a means of letting others into our lives. Many people whom we have known for years take on added dimensions as we discover their talents and creative skills. At one "Festival of the Senses" it was discovered that a local high-school music director was a licensed candlemaker. A woman whom we knew had nursing skills could also play music on a carpenter's saw.

Festival Display Areas

The following suggestions are offered as guidelines for the five display areas.

1. *Sight.* This area is certainly not a "catch-all" category. Art work, particularly two-dimensional art such as paintings, sketches, blueprints, is generally *seen,* so the items not used in the other four categories can easily fit into this display.

2. *Touch.* Included in the touch category are those objects which have an interesting texture: pottery, ceramics, sculptures, and handicrafts such as macrame, weaving, and needlework. Allow viewers to touch the items. Obtain the artists' permission, then with supervision let the small and large hands feel the textures. If possible have a table or display where people can work with clay or other materials.

3. *Sound.* This area is suited particularly for the performing arts, displays of published music, recordings, oral readings, or dramas. Several festivals have scheduled musical and dramatic performances or celebrations during the hours of the open house. If live entertainment is not possible, have taped music or sounds available.

4. *Taste.* Food substances seem most logical in this area. Decorate the tables with holiday or finger foods.

The food can be displayed on attractive trays with sprigs of greenery, ribbons, or holiday ornaments. The items can be used as refreshments toward the end of the open house. If a large-scale refreshment area is not used, at least have some display for "sampling" such as a "taste-test" booth. Ask several people to be prepared to conduct experiments with taste. A person skilled in food preparation (i.e., a home economist or dietician) can excel in this creative endeavor. Blindfold visitors at the festival (cover both the eyes and nose so they cannot see or smell). Allow individuals to sample two foods which are similar in texture and ask them to identify what they have tested. The taste buds have difficulty in distinguishing between certain substances if other senses are limited. Some examples of food to be taste tested are slices of apple and white potatoes; bananas and cooked mashed sweet potatoes; sweet and sour pickles; slices of cucumber and radish; sections of lemon and orange; and slices of cantelope and watermelon.

5. *Smell.* Imagination will make this display fun and unique. A publicized theme can give contributors an idea as to items of art that can be chosen and displayed. One festival advertised a need for creations dealing with "smells of a country kitchen." An area was decorated with antique furnishings, and the contributions that came forth included hot, home-baked bread, homegrown and dried herbs (i.e., dill, mint), newly-churned butter still in the churn, and a warm apple pie placed near a pot of chicken and dumplings! The area should be arranged so that visitors can easily stop and pick up the items to smell or bend down to sniff. By the way, visitors in the "country kitchen" will sometimes wait around until the end of the open house to taste the bread, pie, and dumplings.

These suggestions for areas are offered to stimulate thoughts for displays. The room layout for each display should allow people to flow easily through the exhibits. A floor plan is shown with one arrangement idea. If the food contributions will be eaten, save them for last. Keep the refreshment areas confined to rooms beyond the display areas. Art objects need to be protected from unnecessary soiling. If a large room is not available to hold the entire celebration, use smaller rooms for each of the five categories, plus a refreshment area.

Task Assignments and Preparation

The "leg work" of the festival falls into two main sections with a coordinator to guide the total planning. Depending on the size of the festival, the coordinator may wish to have an assistant. The two sections are: (1) collecting and displaying the art contributions, and (2) publicizing the festival. After the coordinator, his assistant, and the two team leaders are secured, the initial stages of planning can begin. These persons can make basic decisions as to time, date, location, and theme or approach to the festival. Other team members can be added as needs arise.

Reflections on the Festival—The Group Whip

The following group experience will provide persons with an opportunity to reflect on and share their experiences in the festival. No matter how large the group, each person can have an opportunity to share his impressions in concert with several hundred persons present.

Divide the large group into smaller groups of four to fifteen persons. Persons may sit, stand, or turn in their chairs so every person in the group can see the others clearly.

Groups are given questions to discuss. A time limit of five to ten minutes may be imposed on each group to answer

FLOOR PLAN

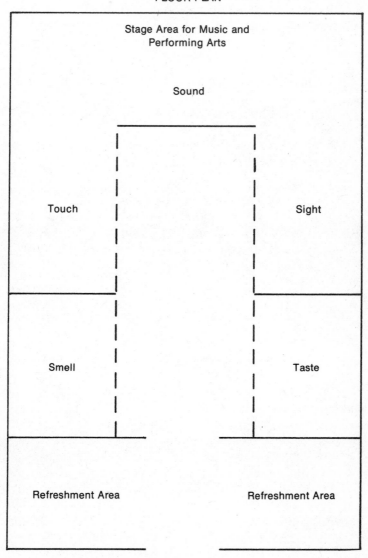

the question. Each person in the group is given a chance to answer quickly in "whipping around" fashion.

Examples of questions:

1. The most interesting thing you experienced during the festival?
2. Which of the five senses seemed to be most familiar to you? Which seemed to be the strangest?
3. Which one of the areas would you like to experience again?
4. What would you have liked to have seen in the festival that was not included?

The "Festival of the Senses" is a model for involving many people in a total experience by using the main body receptors—the senses. The total environment of this celebration deals with sensitivity and awareness, and lets persons use all of their being in a celebrative form. In planning and preparing for this experience, rely heavily on your own sensitivity and creativity.

8 REFORMING RELIGIOUS EDUCATION

"Religion, in one sense, is like baseball or any other form of play or art. The professionals who play in the big leagues render a great service to baseball. Baseball would certainly not pervade our national life as it does, if it were not for these big leagues. But if you want to find the true spirit of baseball in all the glory of a passion you must not go to the big leagues. You must go to the back yard, the sand-lot, the side street, and the school ground. There it is not a profession; it is a passion. When a passion becomes a profession, it often ceases to be a passion. That is as true of religion as it is of baseball. Among the professionals you find a superb mastery and a great technique, but not too frequently the pure devotion. Perhaps in baseball the passion is not so important, but in religion it is all important. A religion that is not passionate simply is not worth considering. Therefore, I say, we need more sand-lot religion. The professional, whether White Sox or Methodist, controls inordinately our baseball and our religion."
—Henry Nelson Wieman, *Religious Education*

Our conclusions are tentative statements about what we are learning from playing games. There are as yet no reliable statistics to substantiate these statements. In a way they are playful probes, hunches, intuitions. They are attempts to articulate things that we see only dimly. The statements suggest a methodology in search of a response. Each statement stands on its own and seeks a reply. Playfully we throw it out to see who will catch it.

But the statements are more than just playful hunches. They are testimonies, shaped from our own experience and taught by the learning environments suggested in this book. It is here that we willingly take a stand. Ultimately, we must choose our methodology or have others choose for us. What we have chosen may be an option for you. Each educational emphasis has its own definition of the roles of teacher and student, its own approach to content, its own definition of learning, and its own answers as to what is most important. These statements reveal how gaming effects persons.

The Training of Professionals

The years of professional preparation develop certain inclinations in persons. At the center is a sedateness. What once was robust and vital now becomes placid and cautious. There is the appearance of having things well under control, a quiet, unruffled approach to life's problems. Because of the years invested in professional training, there is usually an excessive claim to position, dignity, and authority. One's opinions are due more consideration, more attention. There is a tendency toward arrogance and domination, an inclination to exaggerate the importance of one's own views, a willingness to speak for more and more people. Because appearance is more important than experience, playfulness is neither valued nor necessary. Passion, ecstasy, and feeling die a slow death.

Beware of those who cannot play. Those who cannot play cannot laugh at themselves or avoid being possessed by their own importance. Play results in ecstasy. Ecstasy is that absolutely necessary human experience that dilutes arrogance and gives the experience of standing outside oneself, thus seeing everyone and everything in a new way. A person is less "human" without it.

The Need to Control

Professional training develops a need to control the situation. Whether one is planning a workshop or developing a curriculum, an attempt is made to arrange a sequence of experiences that are aimed at predictable results. There is a feeling that "I know things that other people should know, and I can cause something to happen to that person that can be observed or measured."

The need to predict what people will do grows out of a need to avoid uncertainty. The generating of objectives and goals for others is an attempt to cut down on uncertainty.

The fear of losing control evokes a fear of being caught in a mistake. Therefore, good technique is a dominant feature of the professional. A pervasive way of reducing uncertainty is to try to assign probability and predictability to outcomes. The best advertising and public relations schemes are introduced to ensure success. A procedure is set up to bring about good routine in performance. If we can get something to happen in one church, we can cause the same thing to happen in a church on the other side of town. A plan can be developed into a pattern that allows us to produce a hundred more just like it. The language of technique develops—"set it up," "plug it in," "figure out the best procedures," "once we get it going it will take care of itself," "crank it up." A machine technology is transferred to living organisms.

The professional emerges out of a need for control. Instead of learning through the process of trial and error, the professional is brought in to discover, define, and solve problems that would otherwise contribute to uncertainty. The professional has special abilities and trained skills. If he knows something, then he somehow has the power to control it. This need to come up with answers results in a "trained incapacity" to recognize the enormity and complexity of problems. The professional is expected to see order when, in reality, there is no order, to have answers when there are no answers. And even if a person does not have the answers, it is important to pretend that there is enough knowledge to predict the outcome.

Persons in the professions who have adopted an experiential method of learning know these things in their "bones." Gaming, simulations, and other clinical training environments often are turbulent and rich in uncertainty. Nothing can be fully anticipated, and there is risk in any performance. Power is seductive and fickle. It promises much but delivers little. Those who play games know why power and influence must be distributed, why it needs to be given to the many, and why the many need it.

Behavioral Outcomes

Again the issue is, "Who is in control?" The argument made is that the behavior of people conforms to established patterns and therefore is subject to controls that are not part of the person. If one can describe and determine some sort of behavior, one can move people toward that behavior. Each person's response is teacher-initiated and confirmed. Control of the learning situation is external to the learner. Essentially, behavioral methods are authoritarian in nature because learning goals are virtually always framed by persons other than the learner.

Experiential-centered environments assume that people learn slowly when they are forced to adopt a pattern not their own. Leadership attempts to design an environment in which people can choose from a variety of learning patterns and try out new ones if they wish. The advantage of gaming is that a person can be presented with a life situation that allows him to deal with it on his own terms, without having a new sequence interposed on him.

Planning

Planning is directly related to our needs for control. If our teaching methods are to bring about certain results, it is very hard to change the rules as we go along. A good planning process can be essayed and examined, but not predicted. The results are for learning, therefore the plan can be modified or eliminated along the way. The question "Can we do this?" once meant "Do the rules allow it?" The distance from home plate to the left-field fence could not be changed during a ball game. Now, however, planning means we can change the rules. It is now possible to move the left-field fence during the game. We can change the way the game is played as we go along, which is important in the planning process.

People's Religion

There's a difference between professional's religion and people's religion. It is the same difference that exists between professional baseball and sandlot baseball. The rules are the same, but the setting is different. They play for different reasons. The professional plays with a skill and precision of the highest possible quality. It is done for spectators who sit in awe and amazement. Therefore, it is important to put the play into the hands of the most highly competent, physically blessed, experienced, and trained personnel. The professionals come on the scene for five or ten years with eager followings and then fade into obscurity.

The sandlot group plays for a different set of reasons. They play for the satisfying experience of playing—having fun; the quality might be there, but it is accidental and not essential. The important ingredient is that everyone plays. The spectator is looking for quality, and he will pay in order to see it. The participant plays simply for the joy of participation. For the professional the physical setting must be exactly right. Their performance is expected to be smooth and impressive. The sandlot is different. The players are involved with one another—there is no audience.

Learning Methods

The quiet and unverbalized symptoms of boredom are some of the most frequent and devastating reflections of poor methods. The living word sputters out in dead process. Only dynamic methods can carry a dynamic message. Whatever does not touch the core of persons becomes shallow religious sentiment, or is rejected altogether. Because dynamic methods create a certain amount of uncertainty, there are increasing numbers of people who are content with routine. Those who do not find anything very exciting are the first to suggest that something very exciting should not be done.

Learning methods will include the use of complex processes in simple ways. "Systems" is a name that has been given to the work of a small group of persons who have been using cybernetics and computers in the complex process of solving complex problems. Many of these approaches have been impractical or unrealistic in solving the everyday situations that most of us face. We tried to get the computers to do the work instead of understanding how they worked. Understanding how computers work opens up a dynamic new learning process. Experiential learning is an attempt to make systems "soft" instead of difficult and highly specialized. Our everyday situations can benefit from the systems process. ("Think and Rethink," pp. 124-27, is an example of systems theory applied to learning process.)

The church does not need more commercial games that are boxed, packaged, and ready to be brought out at a particular time. What the church *does* need is a more fundamental understanding of the dynamics and significance of the game experience. It must also find ways of utilizing this experience in the communication of the faith. Buying games will not solve the methods problem in the church. A game will become a "sometimes" tool and gather dust for months on the shelves, along with other educational gimmicks.

Ultimately, our methods will be tested by the results in the lives of persons. If our methods are life-giving, they will

increase a person's ability to live with uncertainty and am-
biguity. They will enable persons to trust their experience
in spite of the lack of landmarks on the way. They will result
in continuous human growth and maximizing of potential
self-fulfillment. Our methods will result in a deeper awareness of Jesus and a growth in the fruits of the Spirit that are
mentioned in Galatians 5:22-23. By the fruits of our
methods we shall know if they are valid.

The Generations

The leaders of the new way may well be the
children. The generations need each other. We need our
children as much as they need us. This is the genius of the
life-cycle theory of Erik Erikson—all advances to higher
stages of development and maturity carry forward and re-
state a lower level of development. The mature includes
and restates the child—the more mature, the more
childlike; the more civilized and orderly, the more primi-
tive; the more aesthetic, the more earthy. The more we
grow into Christ, the more we are able to discover the
uncomplicated child in our lives. When we have free access to our own childhood depths, we can enter into
deeper relationships with our own children and with the
children of others. A principle of counseling is basic here.
You will not be able to see and appreciate in others what
you have not learned to recognize in yourself.

The Learning Environment

A true learning environment will be characterized by mutual trust and respect, helpfulness, freedom
of expression, and acceptance of difference. All people will
be involved and accept responsibility for planning and
operating the learning experience, and there will be a
mutual feeling of commitment to its success. All people will
participate actively. Each person will draw heavily from his
own experience.

The emphasis will be on life in the present knowing that memory and hope are both a part of the learning experience. This spontaneity training, the ability to operate here and now, equips a person for a full response to a new situation, or a new response to an old situation. This is an important skill.

The environment emphasizes the learner as a discoverer and maker of his own spiritual meanings. The environment contains objects, people, events, and human situations that stimulate and provoke a person's internal capacities. The leader is a facilitator, an evoker of a person's highly individualized and personal style of learning. Faith is not something that can be poured into a person, but it becomes present to a person if we have enough trust to allow him to explore life in his own way. Trying to control religious outcomes distorts this inner unfolding and revealing of religious meaning.

Witnessing

There is a corporate element in experiential education that proclaims the good news of the gospel. The historical roots of play are in the celebrations of the people. The people of God give testimony by living their faith. The expression of gospel truth is lived out through our whole bodies—through pantomime, games, drama, and theater. This physical realization of experience dramatizes the presence of a living Lord and is a harmonious blending of words, gestures, singing, marching, spontaneous speaking, pictorial designs, and the "beautiful motions" of the whole people.

Worship

There is a transcendent element to experiential education. It is a modern approximation of the biblical festival and feast days. Our play is a deliberate and skilled dramatic picture of what the Christian community is capable of. It is a foretaste of something that is possible, something that might happen, rather than a description of something that has happened. It will picture the followers of the new way (Acts 9:2; 18:25-26). The teachers of the new way will be like Stephen who was charged with speaking against the Holy Place and its customary way of teaching (Acts 6:13). For Stephen, the church was always on the way, never established, settled in, or nailed down. The forerunner was Abraham who kept on moving, always getting up and going in response to the call of God (Gen. 11). The anchorman is Jesus, the pioneer, author, and finisher of the faith (Heb. 12).

The Nature of God

God laughs at our dull and drab need to arrange his program or restrict his performance. He is God of variety, diversity, creativity, innovation, novelty, and adventure. He is a God of fun and games. He journeys with us, battling the forces of complacency, mediocrity, indifference, discouragement, and boredom. Jesus tells us that the Spirit of God blows where he will. We cannot arrange God's schedule or his performance. Try as we may, we are not in control. We simply open our arms to catch the movement of his Spirit and seek to discover the way of moving with it. God did not give us a spirit of fear, timidity, and mediocrity. Therefore, we can take risks; we can let ourselves go; we can take the chance of being turned on to life.

Until He Comes

And so we end as we began, affirming the eternal nature of games. You might say, "Oh, well, it was just a game." But games have a way of pointing to elements that transcend a particular time and place. There are other games in store for us that are played according to kingdom boundaries and rules. Jesus brought the games with him; he invites us to enjoy part of them now with the hope that the best is yet to come. Our hunch is that if you do not like to play games, you will not like spending much time in heaven. So we rejoice in the words from Proverbs 8:30-31 as translated by Moffatt:

> I was with him then, his foster-child,
> I was his delight day after day,
> playing in his presence constantly,
> playing here and there over his world,
> finding my delight in humankind.

Appendix

TEAM-BUILDING EXERCISES

Many team-building games can be developed without the use of any props. You can simulate a relay race, a tug of war, or a taffy pull by using imaginary materials. Give a group an imaginary lump of clay about the size of a person's body and see what they do with it. Ask groups to use their bodies to simulate an automobile, typewriter, wristwatch, or computer. These kinds of activities are most effective if done nonverbally, followed by a short period of reflection and debriefing.

One of the best ways to facilitate team experience is through the building of models. Blocks, Tinker Toys, and various construction sets all contain parts which are to be fit together to make a whole. Parts are to be arranged, fitted, or stacked. Cups, cartons, or cans can be used as blocks. The processes of building models will vary according to the game, but there are some common elements:

1. Individually built structures must connect with the structures that others have built.
2. Structures are built together without planning, but with a time limitation.
3. Begin by planning the structure; however, while the planning is in process no one can touch the blocks. Set a time limit, then build the structure without speaking.
4. Whatever is built will eventually collapse because of faulty planning—one block too many, shaken foundation, or the collapse of another team's connecting structure.

What do people learn? They must work together by matching sizes and making adjustments. What is built must stay together until it is pulled apart. Persons experience a complex system of relationships that sometime succeed but often fail. In other words, "We build it before we build it, to see what to do and what not to do when we actually build it."

Listed below are some materials that can be used for model-building and gaming. Others will be discovered in toy and book stores.

Tinker Toys

Tinker Toys are designed for persons of all ages; and like other construction materials, they can be used to achieve various learning goals.

Lego Construction Blocks

The Lego blocks are used to provide various outcomes such as team-building, competition, and creative expression.

Blockhead!

Blockhead consists of small, colored, wooden blocks of different shapes. The game can be played by persons of all ages, and it adapts to multiple rules and processes.

Resources

THERE IS NO LONGER A FRONT OF THE ROOM

Benson, Dennis. *Gaming: The Fine Art of Creating Simulation Learning Games for Religious Education.* Nashville: Abingdon Press, 1971. A variety of learning games that are excellent examples of redesigning the learning environment. A recording comes with the book.

Carlson, Elliot. *Learning Through Games.* Washington, D.C.: Public Affairs Press, 1970. A survey of simulation-gaming from the participant's point of view. A good starting place for getting the essence and "feel" of the technique.

Church Recreation Magazine is a quarterly publication that is full of ideas for enlivening learning environments. Information available from Materials Services Department, 127 Ninth Avenue, North, Nashville, Tennessee 37234.

Dow, Robert. *Learning Through Encounter: Experiential Education in the Church.* Valley Forge: Judson Press, 1971. His concept of "action parables" is one of the best ways of communicating experiential education in a Christian context. The exercises he suggests are simple with concrete directions. The all-important "debriefing" process is carefully explained.

Geaslen, Jim. *You Game It: An Annotated Topical Index of Simulation Games for Christian Educators.* Order from *You Game It,* Ashland Theological Seminary Library, Ashland, Ohio 44805. A good, inexpensive annotated listing of simulations and teaching games through the summer of 1973 that can be incorporated into Christian education programs.

Hendrix, John. *Nexus: Discovering Spiritual Gifts.* It is available from Baptist Book Stores or Convention Press, 127 Ninth Avenue, North, Nashville, Tennessee 37234. A game that helps persons discover their unique contributions to the church's ministry. The kit consists of a Nexus circle, tokens, and guidance materials.

Jud, Gerald J. and Elizabeth. *Training in the Art of Loving: The Church and the Human Potential Movement.* Philadelphia: United Church Press, 1972. An interpretation of the human potential movement and methods for the local church.

Leonard, George. *Education and Ecstasy.* Delacorte Press, 1968. Education, at best, is ecstatic—the ultimate delight. When joy is absent, the effectiveness of the learning process falls and falls until a person operates fearfully at only a tiny fraction of his potential.

Leypoldt, Martha M. *Learning Is Change.* Valley Forge: Judson Press, 1971. A multitude of learning exercises that are especially helpful in teaching persons how to reflect on their learning experiences.

Minor, Harold D. *Creative Procedures for Adult Groups.* Nashville: Abingdon Press, 1966. Also, *Techniques and Resources for Guiding Adult Groups.* Nashville: Abingdon Press, 1972. A panorama of learning techniques and methods. Only as you experiment with these processes will you be able to determine their experiential and relational value.

Oden, Thomas C. *The Intensive Group Experience: The New Pietism.* Philadelphia: The Westminster Press, 1972. A historical and theological analysis of the encounter-group movement. Especially helpful is the comparison of current small-group processes with the practices of eighteenth- and nineteenth-century religious groups.

Pfeifer, J. William and Jones, John E. *A Handbook of Structured Experiences for Human Relations Training,* Volumes, I, II, III, IV. Also, the 1972, 1973, and 1974 *Annual*

Handbook for Group Facilitators. University Associates Publishers, 7596 Eads Avenue, La Jolla, California 92037. There is more here for your money than from any other one source. Ask to be put on University Associates mailing list.

Simulation Gaming News. Box 3039, University Station, Moscow, Idaho 83843. Subscriptions are six dollars for five issues, and checks should accompany subscription requests. This is the best resource to keep you up to date in the total field of simulation and gaming.

Simulation Sharing Service. 221 Willey Street, Morgantown, West Virginia 26505. Subscriptions are five dollars for ten issues. An ecumenical service to promote the use of simulation/gaming in the church's ministry. Provides reviews of current games, includes suggestions for use.

Spolin, Viola. *Improvisations for the Theater.* Evanston: Northwestern University Press, 1963. One of the earliest books on experiential education. Nontechnical in approach. "Everyone can act. Everyone can improvise.... We learn through experience and experiencing.... The game is a natural group form providing the involvement and personal freedom necessary for experiencing...."

Zuckerman, David and Horn, Robert. *Guide to Simulations/Games for Education and Training.* Available from Information Resources, P.O. Box 417, Lexington, Massachusetts 02173. Lists more than six hundred games and gives suggestions for making effective use of them.

DEVELOPING STRATEGIES

Broholm, Richard R. *Strategic Planning for Church Organizations.* Valley Forge: Judson Press, 1969. A very practical little book that breaks down the complex process of strategic planning for church groups.

Geyer, Nancy and Noll, Shirley. *Team Building in Church Groups.* Valley Forge: Judson Press, 1970. The best thing you can buy for your money in implementing a "team" concept in church groups.

Oden, Thomas C. "Optimal Conditions for Learning" in *Religious Education,* March/April, 1972, p. 131-41. Developing contracts between teacher and students that maximize the learning environment.

Team Building Series. Service Department, Board of Education, P.O. Box 871, Nashville, Tennessee 37202. Four separate units on team building: (1) communicating, (2) diagnosing, (3) leveling, and (4) achieving. Each unit has a cassette recording and workbook that provided understanding of skill and practice in using that skill in a three-hour session.

Reddy, W. Brendon and Kroeger, Otto. "Intergroup Model Building: The Lego Man," *The 1972 Annual Handbook for Group Facilitators.* LaJolla: University Associates Publishers, 1972. A good example of how to use blocks for successful team-building.

PRACTICING THE TEACHINGS OF JESUS

Bradshaw, George. *Cooking at the Table.* New York: Signet Books, 1971. A little paperback of international recipes that delight the stomach and enrich the fellowship.

Capon, Robert Ferrar. *The Supper of the Lamb.* New York: Doubleday, 1969. Cooking and eating that is fun and meaningful and table graces to go along. "O, Lord, refresh our sensibilities. Give us this day our daily taste. Restore to us soups that spoons will not sink in, and sauces which are never the same twice. Raise up among us stews with more gravy than we have bread to blot it with, and casseroles that put starch and substance in our limp modernity. Take away our fear of fat, and make us glad of the oil which ran upon Aaron's beard."

Cochrane, Arthur C. *Eating and Drinking With Jesus.* Philadelphia; The Westminster Press, 1974. A biblical inquiry in why, what, and how men and women eat and drink with Jesus.

Miller, Donald E., Snyder, Graydon F., and Neff, Robert W. *Using Biblical Simulations.* Valley Forge: Judson Press, 1973. An excellent resource in developing simulations around certain key decision-making events in the Bible. The book features duplicate tear-out pages that provide each group with the material needed for its particular role. For advanced groups who are willing to spend some time and effort in simulating biblical experiences.

O'Connor, Elizabeth. *Search for Silence.* Waco, Tex.: Word Books, 1972. For additional resources on how the natural environment teaches us, note Exercise 5, "Contemplative Prayer and the Created Order."

Sugar, Andrew. *Backpacking It!* New York:Lancer Books, 1973. For groups who are really serious about "walking together," this book is a cheap, helpful guide through the natural environment.

Swadley, Elizabeth. *Dinner on the Grounds Cookbook: Favorite Recipes of Famous Baptists.* Nashville: Broadman Press, 1972. A compilation by an old college classmate who has discovered that eating together builds up the household of faith. The first recipe is by Ann Lee, who first taught us that eating together can be a group experience.

Van Matre, Steve. *Acclimatizing.* American Camping Association. Bradford Woods. Martinsville, Indiana 46151. A panorama of individual and group exercises that develop an experiential and reflective approach to the outdoors.

ADULTS AND CHILDREN TOGETHER

Axline, Virginia M. *Play Therapy.* New York: Ballantine Books, 1969. A foundational book on a play environment for adults and children with the children "taking the lead."

Carroll, James. *Wonder and Worship.* New York: Newman Press, 1970. Storytelling that has a message for all ages.

Clinebell, Howard J. *The People Dynamic.* New York: Harper & Row, 1972. This book is especially helpful in developing the concept of growth groups across the life cycle. It also explores the possibilities of children and adults together in groups.

Connect. Designed by Ken Garland and Associates. Made in England by James Galt and Company, Cheadle, England. Distributed by Creative Playthings, Princeton, New Jersey 08540. *Connect* can be played by children and adults. The game consists of 144 small cardboard squares which when connected produce various designs. A large table or the floor is required for the playing area. It easily adapts to new rules and processes.

Middleman, Ruth R. *The Non-Verbal Method in Working with Groups.* New York: Association Press, 1968. Sets forth the idea that people learn through their muscles with hundreds of "nonverbal vignettes" for children, youth, and adults to prove it.

Simon, Sidney B., Howe, Leland W., and Kirshenbaum, Howard. *Values Clarification: A Handbook of Practical Strategies for Teachers and Students.* New York: Hart Publishing Company, 1972. Seventy-nine group experiences that can be adapted for use with all ages. Values clarification is a growing learning model that should receive a wide reception in church education.

Sloyan, Virginia and Huck, Gabe (eds.) *Children's Liturgies.* Washington, D.C.: The Liturgical Conference. 1970. A notebook approach to family worship and liturgy. Excellent methodologies for involving adults and children together.

PLANNING THE FUTURE

Carlson, Adelle. *Harvest: A Fun Game About Retirement.* A card game structured around the decisions persons must make in or before retirement. Can be ordered from a Baptist book store or Broadman Supplies, Nashville, Tennessee.

De Bono, Edward. *New Think.* New York: Avon Books, 1971. Simplifying the use of lateral thinking in generating new ideas.

Koehler, George E. *Futuribles: Training Together with 288 Possible Futures.* This is a deck of cards describing and inventing many different kinds of churches in the future. It is available from book stores, or Service Department, P.O. Box 840, Nashville, Tennessee 37202.

Richards, Lawrence O. *A New Face for the Church.* Grand Rapids: Zondervan Publishing Company, 1970. The new face for the church is the face of *all* the people involved in church planning. Solid biblical frameworks for church goal setting and implementation through consensus.

Schaller, Lyle E. *Parish Planning.* Nashville: Abingdon Press, 1972. Church planning that is theological in method, relational in ministry, and fun besides!

THE SOUNDS OF NOISY ASSEMBLIES

Clark, Stephen B. *Building Christian Communities.* Notre Dame, Indiana: Ave Maria Press, 1972. The author suggests that the church's main objective should be the building of Christ-centered communities by an "environmental" approach which fosters the growth of its members. The environment can contain small groups of twenty-thirty persons and an expanded community of five hundred persons. A community must be able to "potentially" meet *all* the needs of its members.

Forte, Imogene and MacKenzie, Joy. *Nooks, Crannies, and Corners: Learning Centers for Creative Classrooms.* 1972, Creative learning environments for children. A learning center is "any place on earth (or elsewhere) where learning can abound!" Incentive Publications, Box 12522, Nashville, Tennessee 37212.

Madsen, Paul O. *The Person Who Chairs the Meeting.* Valley Forge: Judson Press, 1973. A very practical book by an author who has a "feel" for committee meetings as learning environments.

Sax, Saville and Hollander, Sandra. *Reality Games.* New York: The Macmillan Company, 1972. A lot of ore here for designing group experiences but it will take some digging and refining. Especially helpful are the "community games" which provide help in working with larger groups, organizations, and conferences. Any group, no matter how large, can be divided into core groups, cross groups, and community meetings. The core group is a stable group of four or five persons that provides support, security, and integration of working tasks. Cross groups are made up of one member from each core that meet together to discuss common problems and policies. The community group is made up of four or five core groups, containing up to twenty-four members.

This, Leslie E. *The Small Meeting Planner.* 1972, Practical counsel and training activities on why we hold meetings and what holds them together. Gulf Publishing Company, Book Divisions, Box 2608, Houston, Texas 77001.

Urdahl, Richard. *Plays for Clowns in Christ: Four Short Plays for the Fun of Playing.* Valley Forge: Fortress Press, 1973. A good example of an environmental learning approach through drama. A group may have fun performing these for an audience but the practicing may be more meaningful than the performing.